I0048851

TODAY'S PROFITS TOMORROW'S FREEDOM

The Small Business Owner's Guide
to Thrive Now and Retire Wealthy

RITA ZAPPULLA

First published by Ultimate World Publishing 2019

ISBN
Print: 978-1-925884-19-7
Ebook: 978-1-925884-20-3

Rita Zappulla has asserted her right under the Copyright, Designs and Patents Act 1988 to be identified as the author of this work. The information in this book is based on the author's experiences and opinions. The publisher specifically disclaims responsibility for any adverse consequences, which may result from use of the information contained herein. Permission to use information has been sought by the author. Any breaches will be rectified in further editions of the book.

All rights reserved. No part of this publication may be reproduced, stored in or introduced into a retrieval system, or transmitted in any form, or by any means (electronic, mechanical, photocopying, recording or otherwise) without the prior written permission of the author. Any person who does any unauthorised act in relation to this publication may be liable to criminal prosecution and civil claims for damages. Enquiries should be made through the publisher.

Cover design: Ultimate World Publishing
Editor: Marinda Wilkinson
Typeset and layout: Ultimate World Publishing

Ultimate World Publishing
Diamond Creek,
Victoria Australia 3089
ULTIMATE WORLD   www.writeabook.com.au
— PUBLISHING —

This book is dedicated to both my parents Nicolo and Graziella Zappulla who taught me if I work hard and aim high, I will always achieve my dreams.

To my husband Brien and children Nicholas and Daniel who have supported me on this journey to write my first book and spread the message to my readers to be financially independent and to not rely on the government for their successful retirement. Thanks for your patience and support these past 12 months to make this dream a reality.

To my goddaughter Kerry Farquharson, who when I would doubt myself and want to give up, would encourage me to keep going. For your help in proofreading the book and unshakeable belief in what I can achieve.

TABLE OF CONTENTS

TESTIMONIALS

Our first meeting with Rita was held a few days before Christmas. We were meeting with our bank manager to discuss some business restructuring options prior to my father-in-law leaving for overseas in the next few days. As our bank manager recommended Rita, we phoned her during the meeting to see if we could arrange an appointment. As I explained that we were trying to make some major decisions about our business and our self-managed super fund, Rita dropped what she was doing and came around to our home immediately to join our meeting. She asked very intuitive questions and listened intently before she gave some sound, direct advice that has helped our family know we could move forward financially and restructure the business to provide peace of mind to both sides of the family. From day one Rita's enthusiasm, thoroughness, sound advice and absolute dedication to do her best for us has been undoubtably evident. We are very fortunate to have her as our financial planner and now our friend.

Jane Mitchell,
Nordig NQ Pty Ltd, Cairns

Our firm was one of the lucky recipients of a signed copy of your book as a kind Christmas gift from Rod Harris at TeleBiz in Cairns. As the title and back cover grabbed my interest, I made a point of starting to read it after returning to work yesterday. Having now finished it, I just thought I should let you know how much I enjoyed reading it. Not only was it very relevant to the current circumstances of myself and Jodi, but it was clearly and succinctly written and easily understandable.

It was very reassuring to understand, much more clearly than I previously have, the benefits of having in place our SMSF and how we can make this work for us much more effectively moving forward. As we have all the right tools in place, and now having a much better understanding of many of the options open to us in utilising the fund, and our investments, I'm inspired to take a much greater interest in this side of our affairs. I'm looking forward to focusing more on this during the coming months than I have previously done, and also to improving our investment strategies.

Thanks so much for the great information and the inspiration.

Mark Peters, Peters Bosel Lawyers Cairns

An arms-length referral by another professional is one of the greatest compliments that could ever be given. You are effectively trusting that your clients will be looked after with respect and the highest possible quality professional and personal service available. The risk of a bad experience for a disgruntled client could result in collateral damage back to our practice.

I have been referring clients to Rita for a number of years after meeting her through a mutual client. At that time, I was disillusioned with the financial planning space after receiving considerable negative feedback from clients. Looking back, referring clients to Rita has been one of the best business networking decisions I have made. The feedback from clients has been excellent and the communication between Rita and our office has been proactive for the benefit of our mutual clients. I have found Rita to be honest in her dealings with clients, ensuring that their best interests are a priority over and above any potential financial gain for her business.

Vipiana & Associates are proud of our relationship with Rita and her team at SMSF Strategic Advisors and we look forward to many more years of working together for the benefit of our clients.

Allan Vipiana
Vipiana & Associates Accountants & Advisors Cairns

Having been self-employed for the majority of my working life I have always been very focused on my business, but never seemed to find the time to plan for retirement.

An opportunity came up to purchase the office I was renting, and I looked into buying it through a SMSF. After some research it seemed far too complicated and I had almost given up when I found Rita.

From the first meeting it was very evident Rita had all the answers. I needed to set up a SMSF and borrow to purchase the office, and with a positive and proactive approach Rita made the whole process easy.

Thank you Rita – rather than paying rent each month I am now getting one step closer to retirement.

David Jaunzems,
Cairns Beaches Realty, Cairns

Rita's service is thorough and personalised. She leaves no stone-unturned – and discovered several ways for us to save money rapidly, without sacrificing our lifestyle. Would I recommend Rita? Absolutely!

Mark and Belinda Allen Malanda

I refer clients to Rita because she is very genuine, and she will tell clients what they need to hear, not necessarily what they want to hear. Rita has a huge amount of experience in business, accounting and investing. She not only talks the talk she walks the walk.

Greg Stanton
Barrier Reef Accounting Cairns

We'd been looking for someone knowledgeable & trustworthy to give our finances a financial health check. Our search led us to Rita. We couldn't have been happier. Rita's passion, knowledge, genuine interest and attention to detail, not only put us at ease but also opened our eyes to areas where we needed to improve. She pointed us in the right direction and equipped us with strategies to grow our wealth and plan for retirement. As if that wasn't enough, she also reviewed our insurances and pointed out how we were inadequately covered and updated all our covers. Things we rarely think of in our busy lives. We cannot thank Rita enough for all her assistance. We haven't hesitated recommending Rita to family and friends because we know they will be well looked after.

Dr Sharmila Prakash & Mr Rahul Reddy

Thanks to Rita I have finally started the process of financial planning. She was fantastic to work with. She made everything so easy to understand and her straight forward approach is so refreshing.

I have no idea how these numbers etc work (I find it too confronting and overwhelming).

Rita made sure it was easy for me to understand and has given me excellent strategies to work with. She got me thinking about planning for the future. When someone writes numbers on paper and it's all black and white, we realise how many things we take for granted. She didn't sugar-coat anything, she said what our risk ratio is and what we need to minimise it, financial plans to keep our kids and lifestyle if things went wrong in life.

I was very hesitant to go for a long time, thinking I am not ready yet, but after sitting with her, I realised how wrong I was and I wish I had gone to her earlier, when I was initially referred to her by Rahul.

Thank you Rita for sorting out our insurance and drawing up the financial plan. One step at a time.

Dr Anvitha Rao

Introduction

The inspiration for a book came after I attended the Ultimate 48 Hour Author Workshop by Natasa Denman in March 2018. I have always been passionate about helping small business owners to retire, save tax and be financially independent for their retirement and during her workshop Natasa spoke about the infinite amount of people that writing a book can reach.

With over 25 years of experience working in the accounting and financial planning industry, nothing has frustrated me more than seeing small business owners who have been in business 15 to 20 years and have very little savings in superannuation or their own name to show for all their years of hard work. The most recent client I met was Tim, who was 67 years old and his wife Carol who was 65. Between them they had only $180,000 in super. Their superannuation was also paying a total of $24,000 p.a. in insurance premiums for them both. They still had a mortgage on their business premises of over $650,000. They just could not work out why they weren't getting ahead or see when they would be able to retire.

My main aim is to help small business owners in their early years in business to realise the importance of saving for their retirement. I want to show them if they start within the first five years of the business, it will make a big difference to their lives now and in the future.

My experience is as an accountant and financial planner but also as a business owner. I have owned three businesses to date, and also assist my husband with his legal business.

I was only 26 years old when I went into partnership with Jane Rybarz and so began the business Rybarz Zappulla Chartered Accountants. This was the start of a huge learning curve for me, to find out what it was like to now actually run a business, find the money to pay the wages and rent each fortnight/month and the job I detested most, following up the debtors for outstanding invoices.

At times it felt like a never-ending treadmill I could not get off. Between trying to find new clients, look after the clients we had, do the work and then to get paid for that work, only to then have to start again and look for the next job or client to service so next week we would have the money to pay the wages, the rent…

I hope this book can help you as a small business owner to avoid the predicament of Tim and Carol - and the earlier you start, the better the results will be for you and your family.

The strategies and tips I have provided in this book can be implemented immediately, whatever stage your business is at. Whether you are a start-up with very little cash, or have been in business for several years, there is something for every small business owner.

There are 11 chapters in the book and each chapter stands alone, so if you feel a certain topic grabbing you, you can jump to that section first.

At the end of each chapter there are three action steps you should take, to help you reflect on and implement what was discussed in the chapter.

Please seek professional advice before implementing some of the strategies as they may not be suitable to your individual financial circumstances. The advice I have provided is general advice and not specific to you and your personal situation.

My passion in life is seeing my clients being able to retire and be self-funded and not have to rely on the age pension to live and make ends meet.

The difficulty in writing a book like this is knowing that as soon as Australia has its next federal election or there is a budget announcement in May, some of the information may then be out of date. However, by focusing on the big picture and taking control you can start to improve your retirement in the future. The main messages I want you to learn from this book are:

- start saving early
- save regularly
- plan ahead
- get advice
- know the tax rules and maximise the deductions to your benefit.

Happy reading and I hope you benefit from my advice and the stories I will share. Here's to your business success and a fulfilling retirement.

Chapter 1
Start Now

It's amazing how small business owners figure out how to stretch a dollar as far as they possibly can.

- Marc Veasey

After owning your own home, most Australians have a dream of one day owning their own business and being their own boss. However, the reality of what is involved is often a culture shock when you are starting out. The business doesn't initially meet your expectations in providing you with the income and the lifestyle you want. How many of us dreamed of being our own boss, and the business providing us with the opportunity of not having to work late or on weekends and being able to attend all those school functions for our children. The reality we soon discover is quite different.

So, what is a small business? For the purpose of this book I will use the Australian Tax Office (ATO) definition that a small business is one that has an annual sales turnover (excluding GST) of less than $2 million.

Small businesses in Australia are really the backbone of our economy. We account for 33% of Australia's Gross Domestic Product, employ over 40% of Australia's workforce, and pay around 12% of total company tax revenue. Women are becoming increasingly significant in small business due to the flexibility of working from home and thanks to the internet and NBN, the ability to work remotely and outside of "normal" business hours.

Many of the clients I have worked with have had a turnover of less than $1 million and some would qualify to be called a nano or micro businesses as their turnover is less than $75,000. The size of the turnover does not matter; the issues I have found concerning a client's retirement planning are the same for everyone. Most of them are not putting any savings away for their retirement and as far as they are concerned their business is their superannuation. When they realise that may not prove to be the case and they start saving for their retirement, they all wish they had started sooner and wonder why someone had not told them earlier what to do.

In my 25 years of experience working as an accountant and financial planner, I am constantly disheartened to see so many small business owners who after working 20 to 30 years in their business, have so little saved in superannuation or other personal savings to show for it. Yet the staff they have employed and paid their wages and superannuation for, will sometimes end up with a better quality retirement. Some small business owners only find out when they are about to retire that they are unable to find a purchaser for their business. There is no reward for them at the end for all their years of hard work and the sacrifices they have made.

Many of my clients will often say to me, "It's my business, I want control of my money and the freedom to do what I want with my money and when". I totally understand you need to enjoy life and have the cash flow to keep the business working. But you also need to be providing for your future.

Many Australians are under the mistaken belief that because they pay taxes every year, they will be entitled to receive the age pension when they retire. This might happen in the UK and Europe but not in Australia. It is your responsibility to provide for your retirement.

In Australia, you must first satisfy the asset and income test to see if you are entitled to receive the age pension. Even if you do qualify for the full pension, can you live on the current pension which is a little over $900 per fortnight if you are single or $1,381 per fortnight as a couple?

My focus in this book is to show you that just by starting to make some small changes now and more importantly paying yourself first, you will be able to achieve a comfortable retirement. The younger you are and the sooner you start, the easier it will be to achieve your goals. The result will be an improved lifestyle now with the freedom to do the things you want, when you want, and also a greater choice about when you choose to stop work and enjoy that comfortable retirement.

I also want to give you a better appreciation for superannuation and how it works. I think it's the best kept secret in Australia and I want to explain why you should be using it more. However, with the politicians constantly changing the rules and thresholds most people do not trust it or cannot be bothered understanding it as they cannot see the day when they will actually ever get to use it.

There are some accountants who only see superannuation as something to contribute to when a client needs to get a tax deduction. I was guilty of this when I first started practicing as an accountant in my business in 1996. I tried to look for quick fixes for clients to get a tax deduction and to improve their bottom line and minimise the tax they had to pay. I didn't fully appreciate at that time the long-term benefits for my clients of adopting an annual savings habit of contributing to superannuation.

If you are young, in your mid 30s or mid 40s and just starting out in business, most accountants will tell you this is the last thing you should do when you need to claim a tax deduction. They will tell you that the money in superannuation is trapped, and you can't access it till you are age 60. They may also tell you that the better strategy might be to put any spare money you have into your home loan with a redraw facility or an offset account, so you can save on the interest repayments on the loan and repay the principal sooner. All of these are valid reasons, but the problem is the temptation to then spend this money to either buy a bigger house or go on a holiday or buy new tools and equipment for the business. The spare funds are not then used to build up an investment portfolio, even though the intention was there.

Many small business owners I speak to do not pay themselves any super at all. One of the first strategies I recommend is to pay into super as a minimum 9.5% of the drawings or wages you currently pay yourself from your business.

Most people already don't pay themselves a consistent wage. A recent report by cloud accounting software provider Xero found that 56% of small to medium business owners admitted they either did not pay themselves a wage in their first year or paid themselves below the minimum wage. You would never work for an employer and allow them not to contribute to super on your behalf, so why do you treat yourself differently? You should treat yourself fairly and equally as if you were any other employee in your business and make sure you contribute to your own retirement fund.

Even back in 1926, George S. Clason the author of *The Richest Man in Babylon*, wrote that to be financially successful you need to pay yourself first before the creditors, the rent and the banks, etc.

The vast majority of my clients who start regularly saving small amounts into superannuation, realise it was a lot easier than they thought and wish they had started earlier. They can see their little nest egg growing. If it means you have to delay paying a creditor by a few days or a week then so be it.

But don't neglect yourself and your savings.

The Australian Bureau of Statistics released a report in 2016 which showed that more than half of Australian small businesses close within the first three years of starting operation.

Establishing and closing a business takes a huge monetary and emotional toll on people and their savings and sometimes my clients never financially recover from it. Those three or five years of being in business and not contributing to superannuation can have a huge impact on your retirement savings and your partner's.

A fallacy most clients often think is that "My business is my super. When I retire, I am going to sell my business and that is why I am reinvesting all my profits into the business". Did you know that 84% of businesses are forced to just close the doors and do not get sold?

I have seen several clients over the years who either had to walk away from their businesses as the industry they were in was no longer relevant, or because of new competitors in the marketplace their final sale price was significantly less than they expected. For instance, who would want to buy a video or DVD hire shop these days? There was one client who owned a bus company. They had an offer to buy their business, but decided to wait a couple of years, because they were not quite "ready to retire". By the time they did want to retire, another bus company had flooded the market with cheap new buses, and they were no longer able to sell their second-hand buses and the sale price for their business was significantly reduced.

Even if you can find a buyer interested in buying your business, what price are they prepared to pay for your business? Often clients have had to settle for a reduced sale price which was much less than they were expecting after 15 to 20 years of hard work.

My approach to clients is that if you do sell your business, then this is going to be a bonus golden nest egg to add to your retirement savings and to your super.

Some businesses just won't be able to be sold, because the business is the individual and they are the face of the business. This is often true for the small service providers like bookkeepers, physiotherapists, jewellers and lawyers. Where you can, you should try and systemise and put procedures in place. The easier it is for the new owner to walk into the business and start operating it, the better the sale price you will be able to negotiate.

If you can start delegating and mentoring an employee or implement a succession plan to bring someone in to start taking over the business with the aim of you gradually stepping out, you may actually find you now have a potential buyer for your business.

One of the main benefits of superannuation often overlooked by my clients is the asset protection it provides to your savings. Occasionally businesses may go into receivership or be sued by a creditor and the owner is made bankrupt. The moneys that are in superannuation that have been contributed regularly over a period of time and not just put into superannuation in the last six months, will often be protected under the laws of bankruptcy. The client may have lost the business and their home but at least the savings they have made to superannuation can be relied on to use in the future.

Your business plans, your goals and your visions will be the underlying backbone of making your retirement a reality. In the next five years there is likely to be a glut of small businesses on the market for sale. As 80% of small businesses are owned by baby boomers and they are about to retire, it is expected that there will be an oversupply of businesses for sale, which may then actually push the prices of these businesses down. I want to help you to build your retirement nest egg and if possible, maximise the sale price for your business, so that you can retire when you want and with the income you want.

Your three action steps for this chapter are:

1. Everyone reading this book will be at a different stage of the business cycle. It is never too early or too late to take control and do something. I highly recommend you find yourself a good accountant, bookkeeper or financial planner who you can work with to grow your business and plan for your retirement whether it is in one year, five years or 15 years' time. In the next few chapters I will walk you through goal setting and achieving your dreams, but it is important to surround yourself with professionals you can turn to and trust who can help coach or mentor you along the way.

   Even I as an accountant who understood the numbers, have at times needed to use a coach or mentor to hold me to account and push me to achieve my next goal.

2. As you work your way through the book, define your goal of when you want to retire and how much money you will need. What stage of the business are you at? Are you just starting out or are you five years out from retiring? The strategies in this book can be implemented at every stage of business and even if you are about to retire, it will not hurt to review your goals and look at your budget to see how you are tracking. We all get complacent during the good times, when the business is doing well and the

cash is flowing easily. It's only when things get tight that we start looking for ways to save and wish we had changed our habits sooner.

3. Get a business plan. If you don't have a business plan, then I highly recommend you get one. Now I'm not talking a fancy 50-page document that you have to spend thousands of dollars on. You can do that if you want, but I don't find they work. One of the best strategies I have seen is a one-page document (I have included an example in the appendix section of this book) that just made me focus on what my goals were for this quarter, this year, and for three years' time. I also believe in setting goals for the next five or 10 years – dream big. You need to look at the business plan at least quarterly when you prepare your BAS so you can stay focused to achieve your target. We often overestimate what we can achieve in the short-term and underestimate what we can achieve in the long-term.

By taking ownership and control of your financial future, setting some achievable goals and starting to save for your retirement, hopefully you can now see how simple it is to take control of your own destiny and not be reliant on the government to provide for your retirement.

Chapter 2
Make It Happen

Setting goals is the first step in turning the invisible into the visible.

-Tony Robbins

As a business owner, in your head you will have a vision or goal of what you want the business to be now and in five or 10-years' time. Over time this goal may change, and you will need to be able to adapt so you can make it happen and become a reality. It is important to have a clear goal in mind, and for you, your partner and family to all be on the same page. Decide which goal is important enough to you that it will motivate you to get out of bed each day.

Maybe you want to:

- start your own business

- increase your turnover by 25% in 12 months' time

- increase your profits by 15% in the next 12 months

- retire comfortably in two years' time

- sell your business in the next five years

- make enough money to be happy in retirement.

Start with the end in mind, then you can work backwards to see what actions you need to take to achieve your goal.

Often people struggle to make or set goals or even New Year's resolutions. It is a commonly quoted statistic that approximately 80% of New Year's resolutions will fail by the second week of February. Whether people are trying to lose weight, start saving money or trying to exercise regularly, they seem to set goals that don't stick or become a reality for them.

When goal setting, try not to focus on only one aspect of your life. By including other areas in your life that are important to you, you are more likely to feel fulfilled and balanced. The following categories are the main areas of focus for most people, but you can add in any others which are a priority for you.

- Financial – business and personally

- Health

- Education

- Career

- Family and friends

- Community service

- Travel and leisure time

- Hobbies

For the purpose of this chapter we will only be focusing on your financial goals, but the same concepts can be applied to other areas of your life.

I believe it is important to separate your personal financial goals from those of your business and to ensure that you have separate bank accounts. The success of your business will obviously contribute to your personal success. But you also need to be able to enjoy life and spend money you have taken out as a wage from the business without feeling guilty for treating yourself by spending your personal money.

Goal setting allows you to put a plan in place for the direction you want to head and to become focused on the steps you need to take to make your goals happen.

Breaking your goals down into manageable actions will motivate you to turn your vision of the future into reality. You will get such a great sense of achievement as you reach each milestone and gain self-confidence when you attain your goal. Often it is the journey to achieve the goal that is rewarding and provides the most satisfaction and not the actual goal you have achieved.

There is a common saying I like to refer to:

> *"A dream written down with a date becomes a goal. A goal broken down into steps becomes a plan. A plan backed by action will then become reality."*

How to Set Goals

When setting your goals, it is helpful to use the SMART system which usually stands for:

S – Specific

M - Measurable

A – Attainable (or Action-Oriented)

R – Relevant (or Rewarding)

T – Time Bound (or Trackable)

It is highly recommended that if you are writing your goals down, you write them in the present tense, as if you're already there and have achieved it. This seems to trigger the neurological pathways in the brain to make it think it has happened and therefore you will be more likely to succeed. For example, "it's the 31st of December 2018 and the business turnover is $200,000. I have $40,000 in the bank and I'm now able to enjoy the holidays with my family in Spain".

You will find a template at the back of the book that clearly shows you some steps to follow in setting a goal. I find it important to write down goals and make sure they satisfy each of the steps in the SMART system.

An example of a short-term business goal may be as follows:

> *It is 30 June 20XX, I have acquired three new clients for my consulting business within three months by asking for referrals, launching a social media marketing campaign, and by networking with local businesses. This will allow me to grow my business and increase my revenue.*

> - *Specific: I will acquire three new clients for my consulting business.*

> - *Measurable: I will measure my progress by how many new clients I bring on while maintaining my current client base.*

> - *Attainable: I will ask current clients for referrals, launch a social media marketing campaign and attend two networking functions a week with local businesses.*

> - *Relevant: Adding additional clients to my business will allow me to grow my business and increase my revenue.*

- *Time Bound: I will have three new clients within three months.*

To break this goal down further into actionable steps you might consider implementing some of the following over the next three months:

- Send an email or letter to your existing clients asking for referrals – maybe write to 10% of the database each week over a ten-week period and the following week phone those clients to see if they have any leads or referrals for you. Be sure to build rapport with the client so that it's not just about you getting leads for your business.

- Spend time developing a social media campaign – will you do it yourself or hire someone to do this for you?

- How often will you post to social media – will it be twice a week or daily?

- How will you find your content to use in the social media campaign?

- Which networking functions will you attend each week? At the start of each week make sure you have two events to attend or are connecting with a potential referral partner for drinks or lunch to discuss how you can refer to each other's businesses.

You will not achieve your goals for you or the business unless you take actions and make them happen. Just wishing and thinking about them isn't enough.

People often struggle with sticking to a goal and making it a reality. To overcome this, I recommend breaking your goals down into time frames, such as your lifetime, five years' time, annually, quarterly, monthly and weekly. Then work out what you need to be doing each day to help you achieve that goal. I also highly recommend once a week checking in and reviewing your goals. Review your progress over the past week, month or quarter to see how you are tracking in achieving your big picture goal. Do you need to make changes or is what you are currently doing getting you closer to your goal? Your goals should be somewhere you can see them regularly, so you are reminded of what is important to you to help you stay on track and not get distracted. Don't forget to reward yourself along the way as you achieve some of the milestones that make up the ultimate goal.

You may think, *I've tried this before and it's failed, this goal setting thing just doesn't work for me.* If so, it might be time to think outside the box and try some new ways of achieving your goals. Maybe you need a business coach or mentor to help give you some direction and more importantly hold you to account each week, month or quarter. It can be hard sometimes to stay on track with your goals and to be accountable only to yourself and not someone else.

If a goal is truly important to you, then you will find a way to make it happen. This doesn't mean that life will not throw challenges and obstacles to test you, but when you stay focused and follow your plan, you will achieve it. Two major goals I accomplished in my life (buying my first investment property and setting up my first business) were achieved using this method, so I can attest to it from first-hand experience.

When I was 23 years old, I was living in Brisbane and as I intended to relocate to Cairns, I decided to purchase my first two-bedroom unit/investment property. When I relocated to Cairns 12 months later, I moved into the unit and it became my home. At the time of purchasing the property, I set myself the goal to have the unit paid off by the time I was 30, in seven years' time. While I did not achieve it before my 30th birthday, my unit was paid off within the next six months. In my mind I had made it as I had not reached 31 years of age. How did I do this whilst at the same time going into business and looking at maybe getting married? I just made sure I utilised a mortgage offset account and every spare dollar I had was contributed to the offset account every week, month or as it happened.

I have always aimed high and set myself goals from a young age. I don't know when it started but I always knew I wanted to be self-employed and own my own business just like my parents. I had set myself the goal to do it by the time I was 30 years old.

In 1996 at the age of 26, I was chosen for a four-week Group Study Exchange (GSE) trip with Rotary to Texas, USA. That one-month experience overseas instilled so much confidence in me that when I returned home in May 1996, within two months I had set myself up in the business partnership of Rybarz Zappulla Chartered Accountants with my friend, Jane Rybarz which we began on 1 August 1996. I was not going to wait until I was 30, even though I kept telling everybody on my trip in America that I could not start a business unless I was 30 years of age. What most people do not know is that on 29 May 1996 my mother passed away suddenly and totally unexpectedly. At the time I thought it was a sign for me not to go into business, but my father still encouraged and supported me to go ahead and do this. Life will test you and see how much you really want to achieve your goal.

To help you achieve your goals, some people suggest you do some (or all) of the following self-help techniques as part of your daily routine:

- ten minutes meditation every day

- practice saying affirmations first thing in the morning

- complete a gratitude journal

- create a vision board with pictures of the goals and values you want to achieve.

You will find what works for you and motivates you to stay focused and on track to achieve your goals. For me personally, I have a favourite affirmation that I say and read every morning.

Your three action steps for this chapter are:

1. Sit down and take the time to write out your goals using the SMART concept template at the back of book. What are your goals for:

   - five years,

   - three years,

   - one year,

   - three months,

   - one month and

   - one week?

   Each Sunday night focus on what's important for the week ahead and what you need to be working on to achieve or move you closer to reaching your goal. Try and hold yourself and your family, if applicable, to account. I think it's a good idea to have separate goals for you as an individual, as a family and for your business. Involve your key employees in setting goals for the business that are achievable and attainable together.

2. Monitor your goals. At the end of each week, quarter, or year you should reflect back and see how you've tracked and if you are maintaining your goals. You won't always achieve every goal, but that's where you can learn from it and set yourself new targets. If a goal matters to you, then you will find a way of achieving it and making it happen.

3. Celebrate the wins along the way. Too many times we forget to reward ourselves on our successes and achievements. Make sure you reward yourself at each milestone and when you reach the ultimate goal. It doesn't have to be monetary rewards, it may be something as simple as catching up with some friends for drinks or a movie.

Chapter 3
Take Control

A cardinal rule in budgeting and saving is to pay yourself first.
Once your pay cheque hits your account, wisdom has it that you should
move some amount to savings even before you pay the bills.

- John Rampton

Before we can work out how to save for your retirement, it is important we look at your budget. You will need to do this for both your personal life and for your business.

One of the first things I recommend to clients is to separate their personal money from the business. Whether you are a sole trader, a family trust, or you are operating through a group of companies, keep your personal bank account separate from the business and don't confuse the purpose of each of the accounts. By taking drawings or paying yourself a wage from the business, you can then manage your own personal cash flow. You need to be sensible as to what is a realistic wage or drawings amount you can take out of the business, especially in the early years.

Until you can control what money is coming in and where you are spending it, you really cannot determine how much you can save and plan to move forward. Often clients who have not separated their accounts tend to spend the extra money available, forgetting they need to reserve some of those funds to pay tax, GST, super for their employees and a share of the running expenses for the business. This then creates a situation where you are constantly trying to catch up on payments for the business expenses with the money from the next sales order.

By looking at your budget, you will be better able to take control of your finances and start saving money for things you want to do now (expand the business, attend a trade show or travel) as well as saving for your retirement. When you are in control of your finances it can lead to a better quality of life as you can buy things you want now that are a priority, such as going on holidays or purchasing an investment property. It also provides peace of mind knowing you have saved money for any unexpected emergencies which may arise, and you are on your way to achieving long-term goals like retiring when you want.

One of the first things I recommend you do is establish a cash reserve or buffer, so you are not living pay cheque to pay cheque. However, before you do this make sure you are not living off your credit card, where you are caught in a vicious cycle of paying interest on purchases and not being able to repay the card in full by the end of each month when due. To reduce your feeling of being overwhelmed, and not being in control, your priority should first be to reduce and pay out the credit card in full.

Personal Budget

There are several really good resources that can help you with your personal budget. The Australian Securities Investment Commission (ASIC) website, MoneySmart, has a useful budget planner you can use. I find it's quite easy to fill in and it then downloads into an Excel spreadsheet you can save and amend. There are also several apps you can buy which may be helpful. Track My Spend and the Money Brilliant apps are some of the ones to consider.

Dissect Your Expenses

The first task when doing a budget is setting aside some time to review your bank accounts and credit cards. With most of us living in a cashless society today, you can download your bank statements into an Excel or CSV spreadsheet, making it easy for you to dissect and identify your main expenses. These may include:

- household expenses (rates, electricity, water, gas)

- cost of living for groceries each week

- insurances you pay (health, life, car, home and contents)

- motor vehicle expenses (fuel, registration, tyres, repairs)

- lifestyle (alcohol, cigarettes, takeaway, eating out at restaurants)

- subscriptions (newspapers, magazines, Foxtel, Netflix, Spotify)

- other expenses (gym membership, school fees, holidays).

You should also take note of how much cash you withdraw from your bank account and where you are spending it (lunches, coffees with friends, etc.) and add those expenses into your spreadsheet too.

If you try to review the whole financial year in one go, it can become overwhelming, so I recommend starting with three months and then increasing it to six. You will quickly start to see a pattern of where you are spending your money.

Review Your Expenses

Once you have completed step one and dissected your bank accounts and credit cards, you now need to review those expenses and start thinking if there are any ways to reduce or eliminate them. You may consider saving money by:

- switching to a new provider or plan for your NBN or internet service, mobile phone, etc.

- reviewing your subscriptions including the gym, newspapers, magazines, Netflix, Foxtel, Spotify, etc. Are you still using them, and do you still need them? It may not seem much but each of these at $10 a week or month quickly add up to significant potential savings of $520 p.a. or $120 p.a. Do this for any subscriptions you have for your children too – I quickly found my children had outgrown several of the software programs which I had subscribed to a year earlier.

- reviewing your insurances for your car, home and contents, life insurances and health fund every couple of years.

- reviewing your home loan and the interest rate you are paying. Some of my clients who simply asked their bank for a better interest rate and advised them they were shopping around, were able to reduce the interest rate by 0.5% without the need to move to another bank.

Making the Tough Decisions

Being in business in the first few years is about making sacrifices and deciding how much do you really want this business to work and be a success. This is now the time to decide what is a priority and a need and not just something nice to have and want. Look for expenses you can eliminate or reduce so you can start saving money.

If you find yourself living pay to pay, review when the big expenses are due, for example, rates, electricity, gas, insurances and school fees. Add up these expenses for the year and then divide the total into a weekly or monthly amount. Consider paying a set amount off each of these accounts weekly or monthly or alternatively set up a separate bank account and each pay you transfer a set amount to this account for the sole purpose of paying these bills as and when they are due. This should reduce your shock each time a bill arrives. This will take a little while to implement and for the benefits to flow through but stick with it and it will be worthwhile.

When setting a budget, you need to be realistic and allow an extra buffer of 10% for those emergencies and hidden things that you might have forgotten.

If at the end of each month there is no increase in your personal or business bank accounts, then you know something needs to change. This is the time to start saving money and you can do this by:

- reducing your credit card debt if applicable

- parking money in your home loan only if it has an offset or redraw facility so you can build a cash reserve for a rainy day or emergency

- start putting some money into superannuation for your retirement.

Your personal budget is important because we need to know what income the business has to generate to provide you with the lifestyle you want. If the business after several years can't provide you with this necessary cash flow, then you need to look at ways for the business to improve its sales or reduce its expenses to give you what you need. Or alternatively, consider the difficult decision to sell the business and become an employee again.

In the appendix section at the back of the book, there is a Personal Budget Planner template for you to use and this can also be downloaded from our website.

Business Budget

Preparing a budget for your business is a bit different. If you have already been in business, this helps, because you can review the results from the profit and loss statements from the prior years and analyse the expenses to see which are significant in the running of your business and which month these expenses are generally payable.

If you are just starting out in business, then it is also good for you to think about what expenses are likely to happen and what month these projected expenses will need to be paid.

It's important to analyse your profit and loss statement, your sales and the variable and fixed expenses for the business each month. Variable expenses are the costs of producing or selling the product or service you provide. If you produce an item, it might be the costs that go into manufacturing the item, e.g. the materials, wages to produce the item and the freight. This is also often called the costs of goods sold. If you are in a service industry, such as a plumber or electrician, it might be the wages to do the job plus any materials specifically for that job.

What you want to monitor here is the gross profit margin each month. To calculate the gross profit margin, you will need to know your sales and cost of goods sold figures from your profit and loss. The formula you need is as follows:

$$\text{Gross Profit Margin} = \frac{(\text{Sales} - \text{Cost of goods sold})}{\text{Sales}} \times 100\%$$

The higher your gross profit margin the better it is for your bottom line and the amount of net profit you get to keep.

If you sell a number of different products another exercise for you to do is analyse the gross profit margin for each of the products or service lines you sell and provide. You may be surprised to find the best gross profit return may not be from the item you sell the most.

You will also have costs that are called fixed costs. Whether you sell one item or 100, you will still have to pay that expense. Normally this would include expenses like rent, insurance on your building, loan repayments or hire purchase repayments on equipment and often some wages costs are also fixed. It doesn't matter whether your business is producing anything, you still must pay those expenses for that period.

In business it is important you set the time frame for the budget, so you can start to forecast when you expect the most sales to happen and when you expect the biggest expenses are due to be paid. Some clients work on financial years and others prefer to do it by calendar year.

The longer you have been in business, the easier it is to review the profit and loss statements over several years and start to see a cycle for your business. You can then more easily predict in which month or quarter your major expenses are occurring or when your turnover should increase or reduce. By having this knowledge and by being prepared, you can then better manage the cash flow and make your business more efficient.

It allows you to also determine what level of turnover/sales you need to be producing to be able to cover those expenses, pay yourself a wage and still leave a profit in the business.

Also, if you know when you are busy or when there's going to be a lull in your cash flow, you can put funds away for those quiet times. For instance, my husband and I know in October and November each year, we need to generate extra invoices, so we can reserve the extra funds to pay the wages over the Christmas period and help our cash flow in January till we start back and can bill the next lot of work.

By reviewing the sales and expenses monthly, you can quickly see if there is going to be a cost blow out or sales downturn which is contrary to your budget or expectations. This means you can stop the potential problem early enough to avoid any issues with your cash flow.

If the business is about to expand and go through a growth spurt, before committing yourself to any significant fixed costs, maybe look at alternatives to manage these expenses. For example, instead of employing new full-time staff, maybe hire them as casual/part-time employees or alternatively subcontract the work at this stage.

Also, if you will need new equipment or regularly upgrade your business equipment, consider using hire purchase or leasing rather than outlaying the full cost to purchase it. This will minimise the impact on your cash flow and cash reserves.

You want to ensure the increase in new work is consistent and sustainable before outlaying significant money and resources to accommodate the expansion.

Once the growth of the business and the expansion is permanent, then you can look at making some of these costs fixed. Whether you do buy the equipment or employ full-time staff, each business needs to consider what will work for them and their cash flow.

I have seen over the years too many businesses grow and expand too quickly and not control their expenses to the extent they end up closing down or going into receivership. I want you to avoid this happening to your business. Again, having a good accountant to work with who can help you plan for this next phase for your business is vital.

I cannot stress enough the importance of monitoring and reviewing your performance against your budget monthly, quarterly and yearly. So many people set a budget but then do not make the time to review it and learn ways to improve their business and to save money.

Your three action steps for this chapter are:

1. Dissect the expenses and the cash flow for your business for a 12-month period and for you personally a minimum six-month period but preferably one year. Download an app or do the MoneySmart spreadsheet from the ASIC website if that will make your life easier.

2. Review these expenses and see where savings can be made personally and in the business. Each year try to look at ways to reduce your total expenses by 10% in the business. Analyse

your profit and loss expenses line by line, and by finding savings of 1% across several expense items you will achieve the 10% savings goal. It might only be 1% on your advertising, Facebook or yellow pages marketing, office supplies and stationery, telephone and internet bills and staff overtime – but it all quickly adds up.

3. At the start of each year, set a budget for the business and you personally. Monitor the budget monthly, quarterly and annually and make changes if necessary. By forecasting and budgeting for your business, you will be able to see when the lulls will be and plan for extra cash flow and funds in the business during that period.

Chapter 4
Know Your Numbers

A small business can survive for a while without making a profit,
but if its cash flow dries up, the impact is fatal.

- Theo Paphitis

When starting out in business, one of the first concepts we often struggle with is the difference between the profit and loss statement and a cash flow statement.

A cash flow statement will integrate what you have prepared in the budget and it can be one of the most important tools in managing your finances. It will be tracking when the money is coming in and out of the business and the estimated balance in your bank account. It will help you realise how quickly your debtors are paying you and the length of time it takes you to pay your creditors. It is an effective tool to monitor and control expenses.

On the other hand, your profit and loss statement will show the net profit for your business, how it is tracking and if there are any surplus funds at the end of the month, quarter or year you are reviewing. A profit and loss statement will list your sales and your expenses and really, we are only looking at things from a tax point of view. If you prepare your BAS quarterly (or monthly depending on your business turnover), the profit and loss statement will show you if the business is making money or losing money. Sometimes a loss is not a bad thing. You may have bought extra stock in October in anticipation of the sales you are expecting in the lead up to Christmas in November and December, which is why just looking at one month in isolation can be misleading.

The problem for some business owners is they see a profit at the end of the month or year and their accountant tells them they need to pay tax, but the cash that is physically in the bank account doesn't correlate with the profit they made. They start to get frustrated and confused by what the numbers really mean.

It is critical that you grasp these different concepts and understand what affects them. When you know how the finances work and the timing of your sales, cash receipts and expenses, you can be better prepared, and avoid any unexpected surprises. It's also important you understand the mechanics of your business and know how long it takes from the time you first get an order to:

- start work on a job

- make and produce the item or deliver the service

- receive payment from the customer.

Often clients don't realise that from when you first get the order to when you actually get paid by the client can be anywhere from 30 days to 120 days or even longer at times. By controlling and reducing this to a shorter time frame, you can better manage your cash flow. Developing efficiencies in your processes will hopefully improve your profit too. If you are expecting a profit this financial year, you should look at ways to minimise your tax payable, while still watching your cash flow.

Another common mistake I see is people spending money just to get a tax deduction on things like vehicles or new equipment for the business which are nice to have but not really necessary at this time. There is absolutely no point spending money just to get a tax deduction if it is then going to impact on your business cash flow. Sometimes you are better off paying the 30% tax and keeping the remaining 70% to save and spend in the future when it is really needed.

Paying Your Taxes

Many new business owners often overlook or forget to put money away for tax in the first year of operation. I often advise clients to set aside in a separate bank account or contribute to their home loan which has a redraw or offset account 20% of the turnover for that week or month. Then, in 18 months when they prepare their first tax return and need to pay the tax bill, the business is buffered by having this reserve already set aside. Parking funds in your home loan offset or redraw facility allows you to also reduce the interest you will pay on this loan and reduce the principal outstanding on the loan faster. It may not seem much, but this can help to substantially reduce the term of your loan.

Many business owners also forget to put aside funds for the Goods and Services Tax (GST). GST is the 10% that you collect on behalf of the government from the turnover you invoiced your clients. Again, if you are having trouble controlling the cash flow and there are not enough funds in your bank account to pay your BAS when it is due, it may be advisable to set up a process of transferring 10% of every sale to a separate bank account/home loan so you are able to pay the quarterly GST to the ATO as and when it is due.

Often businesses who employ staff may struggle with finding the cash to pay the monthly or quarterly PAYG and 9.5% superannuation guarantee charge for their staff's wages. Again, allocate funds to a separate bank account for these taxes and employee expenses each week or fortnight when you do your payroll. The introduction of single touch payroll in Australia may remove this problem for some small business owners.

A common complaint I hear from business owners is that there is never any money in the bank account. If you find yourself in this position it is important you sit with your accountant or bookkeeper and review your profit and loss and reconcile with the bank account where you are spending the money.

Sometimes the expenses are legitimately for the business but other times it might be money spent on holidays or other personal expenses like upgrading the car or home improvements.

If money was spent on the business, like buying equipment or a new vehicle, then all is not lost as it is recorded on the balance sheet as an asset. Although you do not actually get the full tax deduction in the first year you bought it, the good news is you should be able to claim depreciation over a couple of years. Your accountant will advise you what the ATO recommends as the depreciation rate for this asset. Therefore, on the profit and loss statement for the first year you will see a reduced amount as depreciation expense and for the several years following. For example, on July 1 you bought a piece of equipment worth $30,000. The equipment has a life expectancy of five years in the business before you will need to purchase a new one. On your balance sheet it will show the asset of $30,000, but in your profit and loss there will be a tax deduction for this year and the following five years of $6,000 p.a.

Learn to work with a good bookkeeper or accountant who can help you understand and appreciate the timing of your expenses and revenue and what you can do better to monitor and control the cash flow you need to be able to pay your bills. I know these concepts are often not easy to understand, especially if you hated maths at school. However, for the success of your business and your financial future you need to have a basic appreciation of the things which will impact on the profit for the business and the taxes you will need to pay.

Turnover/Profit

A phrase often used in business is: "Turnover is vanity, profit is sanity and cash flow is king". Most people and the media focus on the turnover and think it is awesome to say I have won a job worth $200,000 or I have a turnover of $1 million. But what they forget to mention are the expenses to be paid to deliver that job and what they really should be monitoring is the actual profit made. Recently one of my clients was tendering and winning significant government jobs but they just could not work out why there was never any money in the bank. Their accountant sat down with them and reviewed their quoting process and looked at **ALL** the costs involved in delivering a job. They discovered the client had not allowed for any of the fixed costs in their quotes such as worker's compensation, insurance on the building, electricity, etc. No wonder they were winning the jobs, they were underquoting!

Furthermore, the client discovered within each job they had won, their staff were not being monitored or working as efficiently as they could. The staff were taking longer than necessary and being paid overtime wages to deliver the job by the due date which meant reduced profit for the business owner.

That is why it is imperative to review your profit and loss, if not weekly then monthly and definitely when you do your quarterly BAS. Any cost overruns or inefficient work practices can be identified early and the financial cost to your business minimised. Otherwise it may not be until 12 to 18 months later when the tax return for the business is prepared, that the problem is found and rectified.

It is therefore important to stay on top of when your expenses are due and where the cash flow will come from to pay for them.

Debtors

Equally as important is monitoring how long your debtors are taking to pay their invoices. Invoices need to be raised as soon as a job is completed. Do not just wait till the end of the month. Debtors should be given 30 days from the date of the invoice and not from the end of the month the work is completed. Monitoring your debtors to make sure they are paying your invoices within the agreed terms is important to help manage your cash flow. If you don't like doing this job, then hire someone to follow up and remind debtors their invoice is overdue and needs be paid. Most accounting software today allows you to set up automatic reminders for unpaid invoices when they are overdue, but this means you need to be processing daily when invoices have been paid.

It is very easy for you to become an unofficial bank for your customers, by effectively financing the cash flow requirements for their business. A recent government report showed that most small businesses in Australia have their debtors out to 120 days and the worst payers were big business. This should be reduced to no more than 30 to 60 days. If a customer has not paid you and is sitting at 60 days do not do any further work for them until the invoice is actually paid. Make sure the money is in the bank, do not just take their word they will by paying you "in tonight's creditor run".

The Pareto Principle, which is often called the 80/20 rule, states that 20% of the products will bring in 80% of the revenue. So, try focusing on those things that work in your business that are going to give you the best results and generate the most revenue. You should also look at who are your best customers, because you may be surprised to find that 20% of your customers will actually give you 80% of your sales. This gives you plenty of incentive to look after them and do all you can to make sure they keep coming back and buying from you.

Sales Quotes

It is important you control the sales quotes and tenders you lodge for your business. Sometimes a business can grow too quickly, and if the growth is not done in a structured or controlled manner it can lead to shattered dreams, loss of money and in the worst case, liquidation or bankruptcy.

If your business is expanding, you need to have systems and procedures in place to control the cash in and out of the business. To help control the expenses as discussed in Chapter 3 consider employing any new staff during the expansion period as part-time or casual employees or sub-contractors, and instead of buying the equipment, you may want to look at using leasing or a hire purchase agreement.

Your three action steps for this chapter are:

1. In the appendix section, you will find a template for a cash flow statement and a profit and loss. You should look at ways to either increase your sales, even by 1% to 5% and then ways

to reduce your expenses, so that by increasing your profit, you can have a positive effect on your bank account and your cash flow. It is too easy for small business owners when they see money in the bank, to think they should spend it, and deserve to reward themselves. For the first 12 months to two years, I advise business owners, to be disciplined and not to spend any of the "spare cash" until their first tax return for the business is prepared and lodged and they know their actual tax bill for the current year and following year as advised by the ATO or their accountant.

2. Review your debtors and your cash collection terms and see what you can do to improve them. Do you need to be asking for 50% payment up front if you are producing items that have a significant material outlay/cost for you? Or change your billing terms to allow you to do interim invoices, if the job goes beyond a month or two? You want to minimise the risk of becoming an unofficial bank for your clients.

3. Monitor your tax bills. For the first year's tax return if you are self-employed, watch out for the tax bill due in 18 months' time. Also ensure you are reserving for the GST, PAYG and superannuation payable on your staff's wages. Once you fall behind on these payments, it can become a vicious cycle of accruing interest on late payments or needing to enter into a payment plan with the ATO.

Chapter 5
Don't Give It All Away

I am not evading tax in any way, shape or form. Of course, I am minimising my tax. Anybody in this country who does not minimise his tax wants his head read. I can tell you as a government that you are not spending it so well that we should be donating extra.

- Kerry Packer

There are two certainties in life - death and taxes. We can't control or know when we're going to die, but we sure can make a difference in minimising the tax we pay in our lifetime. We all need to pay tax. The taxes that we pay help keep the country running by supporting the health and education system, emergency services, and maintaining the roads and infrastructure we use so we can live in an efficient society.

It is important you understand which taxes you are required to pay and how you can minimise them. This allows you to save money which can then be used to contribute to growing your business or saving for your retirement.

I strongly believe in working smarter and not harder. I like to show clients strategies to reduce their tax payable each year whilst also saving for their retirement and decreasing the number of hours they work.

The ultimate result I want you to achieve (based on current legislation) is to be retired and receiving a regular income which is tax-free. This goal has been achieved by so many of my clients who chose to spend their last five to 10 years of working, planning on how to minimise their annual tax bill and save for their retirement.

Tax and Your Business Structure

One of the first considerations in saving tax is considering what your current business structures and if it needs to be changed. As the business grows it might be time to transfer from a sole trader to a company or to a family trust. The different structures often used in business are:

- sole trader

- partnership

- company

- trust.

Sole Trader

When you first start out in business most people start out as a sole trader which means they operate the business in their own name. This is the simplest structure to use and there is minimal set up costs. They are taxed at the same rate as an individual. A disadvantage to consider is this business structure does not provide you with any asset protection in the future should something go wrong in the business. Your personal assets could be seized by the bank or your creditors. Also, there are limited options for you to minimise tax other than claiming tax deductions.

Make sure you know the tax rate you are currently paying. As at 1 July 2018 the tax rates for individuals are as follows:

Taxable Income	Tax Payable * Residents	Tax Payable * Non-Residents
Up to $18,200	Nil	32.5%
$18,201 - $37,000	Nil + 19%	32.5%
$37,001 - $90,000	$3,572 + 32.5%	32.5%
$90,001 - $180,000	$20,797 + 37%	$29,250 + 37%
Above $180,000	$54,097 + 45%	$62,550 + 45%

*Plus Medicare levy

Partnership

Often a husband and wife starting a business together may consider using a partnership structure. A partnership can consist of two or more individuals, companies or even family trusts working together to run a business or own an investment asset. The partnership must lodge its own tax return and each partner will be required to pay tax on their share of the partnership's net income. If the partners are individuals the individual tax rate will apply to them and they may also be required to pay PAYG instalments, in the same way as a sole trader.

Company

As the profit in your business increases to about $100,000 it may be advisable to transfer the business to a company structure. A company is a separate legal entity and is responsible for paying income tax on its profits at the company tax rate. There is no tax-free threshold for companies and small companies are generally taxed at 27.5%.

Operating your business as a company will provide you with a better level of asset protection compared to a sole trader, even though you will have other legal duties and responsibilities as a director or shareholder of the company. However, a negative about owning assets in a company is if it sells an asset and makes a capital gain it does not have the benefit of the capital gains tax 50% discount concession available to you as an individual.

Trust

A trust is an arrangement, defined by law, where someone or a group of people are responsible for assets for the benefit of another group of people. The people who administer the trust are known as trustees. Anyone entitled to receive a distribution from the trust is listed in the trust deed as a beneficiary. A trustee must lodge an annual trust return. The trust is not liable to pay tax if it distributes the income each year to the beneficiaries. Prior to 30 June, you would meet with your accountant to do some tax planning and sign a minute/election as to who is to receive a trust distribution and what amount or percentage of income that person will receive for that financial year. With proper planning this will allow you to minimise the total tax payable on the trust income.

If the beneficiaries are individuals, they will be assessed for tax at their personal tax rate but if it is a company then it will be taxed at 30%. If the income is not fully distributed to the beneficiaries, the trustee will need to pay tax on the undistributed income at the highest marginal individual tax rate of 45% + 2% Medicare.

Summary

Which business structure is suitable for your business when you are starting out or as it grows should be something you discuss with your professional advisors. Before you move from one business structure to another you want to be careful you do not trigger any unnecessary capital gains tax or stamp duty. Talk to your accountant and lawyer to make sure you have considered all the pros and cons of transferring to another legal structure. Saving tax should not be the only reason you do something. Below is an example if the business made a taxable income of $150,000 how it would be taxed within each of the tax structures discussed above.

	Individual	Partnership 2 people	Trust 4 adult beneficiaries	Company
Business Income	$150,000	$150,000	$150,000	$150,000
Income – Individual names	$150,000	$75,000	$37,500	
Tax payable per person*	$43,132	$15,922	$3,734.50	
Total Tax Payable	$43,132	$31,844	$14,938	$41,250
Average tax rate on $150,000	28.75%	21.23%	9.96%	27.5%

*Excludes Medicare levy

Different Taxes in Business

Being in business there are numerous different tax obligations you need to be aware of which may affect your business. As your business grows you should discuss with your accountant if you need to plan or consider any of the following taxes which may impact the business' future viability.

a) **Goods and Service Tax (GST)**. If your business has a turnover of less than $75,000 you do not need to be registered for GST. Many businesses prefer to be registered so they can claim the GST credits on their expenses and be prepared for when the business grows beyond the $75,000 turnover threshold, so it will not be such a big increase in price for their customers in the future.

The GST is basically a broad-based tax of 10% on the majority of goods and services sold or consumed in Australia. If your business is registered for GST, you need to charge your customers GST, and then pay this to the ATO by lodging a Business Activity Statement (BAS). In addition, when you purchase goods or services to use in your business which you have paid GST on, you can then claim back a credit for the GST you have paid.

A BAS is usually prepared quarterly but some businesses need to do it monthly. If your turnover is low you can elect to lodge the BAS and pay the GST annually, however, be aware it can be difficult on your cash flow if you have not been disciplined all year to set aside these moneys.

b) **Fringe Benefits Tax (FBT).** This is a tax an employer will pay on certain benefits they provide to their employees or relatives and associates. This benefit is usually in addition to, or part of, their salary or wages package. The most common benefits provided are a motor vehicle for personal use, mobile phone, or computers and laptop for home.

FBT is separate to income tax and the FBT year runs from 1 April to 31 March of the following year. Your accountant will be able to help you deal with the necessary paperwork and strategies to minimise the effect on your business.

c) **Superannuation Guarantee Contributions (SGC) and PAYG**. As an employer you are required to remit superannuation (also known as super) of 9.5% of the employee's gross wages to their nominated superannuation fund to provide for their retirement. If an employee earns less than $450 in a month, then no super needs to be paid for that employee for that month. You must pay the SGC at least four times per year, by the quarterly due dates of 28 January, 28 April, 28 July and 28 October. However, from a cash flow point of view I prefer to pay the super for my staff each month.

As well as paying super for your staff you need to remit to the ATO the PAYG deducted from the gross wage you paid your employees. The ATO annually provides a schedule of how much needs to be deducted from each employee's pay when you pay them. The size of your payroll will determine if this is to be remitted to the ATO quarterly or monthly. Some businesses prefer to pay this monthly to assist with their cash flow. As your business grows you may also need to pay payroll tax. The amount of payroll tax varies state by state and you should talk to your accountant to see when you need to allow for this additional expense or what strategies you can implement to reduce or even delay having to pay it.

You need to be aware of these taxes and charges not only because you are legally required to pay them, but because they will impact the profit and cash flow of your business. You may need to increase your prices as the business grows to ensure you can absorb these costs and still have a profit.

Paying Your Tax Bill and Cash Flow Management

Before we focus on retirement, let's focus on those of you who may have just started out in small business and are about to get the biggest tax shock of your life. During the first year or two in business there may not have been much profit, but in years three and four everything is starting to come to fruition, the marketing is working and now you are starting to show a decent profit which also means you will have to pay tax. You have cash in the bank, and it is tempting to finally reward yourself and spend some of it. But **STOP!** Before you do that, consider your upcoming tax bill.

Most small businesses/individuals are not prepared for the double tax hit when they have their first "big" profitable tax year. Prior to now you may have paid some small tax bills. But as the business has grown, so has the profit and the amount of tax you need to pay. Most businesses, if they are using a tax agent, do not need to lodge their tax return until March or April of the following year (nine to 10 months later). For example, the tax return for the financial year ended 30 June 2019 is not due to be lodged with the ATO until March or April 2020 and the tax bill paid in May/June 2020. Many businesses are unaware though that now the ATO will estimate their tax bill for the following financial year (in this case the 2020 financial year) and expect this tax instalment to be paid by end of July 2020. So, within a short 2 to 3-month period you will need to pay a second large tax bill. I call this the double whammy tax year. It is essential you set aside the cash, so you can minimise the shock on your bank account and savings account when you need to pay these tax bills.

This problem could have been minimised if instead of leaving your tax return to be completed in March 2020, you lodged it in July/August 2019, as you would then be aware of the "damage" for the amount you owe the ATO. If you lodged your tax return in August 2019, the ATO will then notify you of the quarterly PAYG instalments. Instead of paying one large amount in July 2020 you can now pay smaller amounts quarterly in September, January, April and July of the following year. This is often more manageable for your cash flow and your sanity.

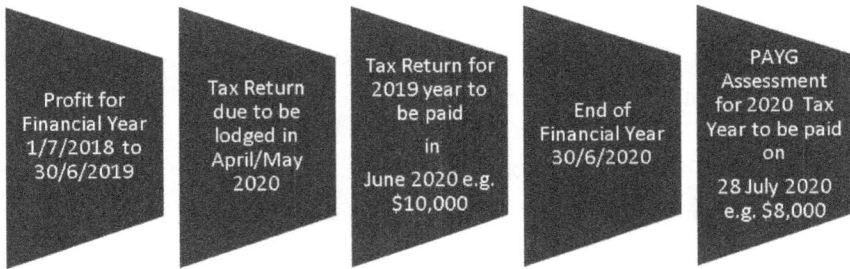

| Profit for Financial Year 1/7/2018 to 30/6/2019 | Tax Return due to be lodged in April/May 2020 | Tax Return for 2019 year to be paid in June 2020 e.g. $10,000 | End of Financial Year 30/6/2020 | PAYG Assessment for 2020 Tax Year to be paid on 28 July 2020 e.g. $8,000 |

I often recommend clients in their first year put 20% to 30% of their profit aside in a separate savings account or into a home loan with an offset/redraw facility if they have one. By doing this, when it is time to lodge the tax return and pay the tax bill, they will already have the money allocated and ready. If they have "over" saved the money, then it is a bonus for them to spend or save. This will minimise the need to find a lump sum amount to pay in tax. If you have a home loan set up with a redraw or offset account, the added benefit of this strategy is you are reducing the interest you will pay on the home loan, the principal loan amount outstanding and effectively, the term of the loan.

Tax Planning

Finding time to do tax planning each year is critical to your business success. In April or May each year you should meet with your accountant once your BAS for April of that year is completed and review the business' performance over the past nine months. Even if you do not think you had a profitable year, just spend the time to review and check things. Often in previous years, clients who thought that financial year was not going to be profitable, would occasionally receive a significant sales order in May or June. The clients who were switched on phoned me for a follow-up meeting in June to review and decide whether to put some money into superannuation or what other strategies they should implement to reduce the tax bill for the business and them personally. This ended up saving them a significant amount of tax that they did not need to pay.

The clients who are "too busy" to phone, 10 months later regret not making the time as not only could they have reduced the tax they need to pay but they have also missed an opportunity to save for their future or retirement.

Paying for an hour or two of advice upfront will generally set you up for the year ahead and allow you to save on tax significantly.

You need to stay up to date and learn to use the current rules for your tax advantage. I constantly see businesses pay tax which could have been minimised – they just give away their hard-earned profit and cash. For instance, in the last two to three financial years, the government has allowed a 100% write off on any assets used in the business which cost less than $20,000. Many of my clients have taken advantage of this to revamp their IT or phone systems, computer software and even buy new vehicles for their business. This tax benefit is expected to cease on 30 June 2020.

When doing your tax planning it is also a great time to review your personal situation and put some money into superannuation for yourself. You will be able to claim a tax deduction and reduce the tax you will pay in the business whilst providing for your retirement, thereby receiving twice the benefit from the one amount you paid. The benefits of superannuation will be further explained in Chapter 6.

Capital Gains Tax

Another important tax consideration for small business owners is capital gains tax (CGT). As a small business operator, you will most commonly make a capital gain or loss when you sell one of the assets used in your business, such as the business premises, or when you sell your business, for example goodwill.

The good news is there are a number of CGT tax concessions only available for small businesses and working with a good tax accountant who understands the CGT rules ensures you minimise the tax you will pay on the sale of your business or premises. I will discuss these options further in Chapter 9 when you are ready to sell the business.

Your three action steps for this chapter are:

1. Find out which items are tax deductible for you and your industry and maximise your tax deduction claims. Have a meeting with your accountant and determine if you qualify for other deductions. Are there any special rules introduced in the latest budget that you may qualify for e.g. the $20,000 immediate write-off?

2. Tax planning. It is important you meet with your accountant and look at last year's tax returns and start reviewing your tax

planning for this financial year. See if there is anything you should have changed or could be doing differently to save tax and make your business more profitable. Make it a priority prior to 31 May to identify what you need to do to minimise your tax bill for this financial year.

3. Maximise the amount you can contribute to superannuation and claim as a tax deduction each year. Why pay tax unnecessarily? If you are employed in the business, first determine what super contribution the business has already paid on your behalf and if there are funds in the bank account surplus to your needs consider contributing to superannuation an amount up to the maximum allowable of $25,000. You may only be able to contribute $2,000 or $5,000 extra a year but it will all make a difference to the tax you pay and your retirement savings in the future.

Chapter 6
Savvy Super

There are times when the presence of more choices can make us choose things that are not good for us. For me the clearest example is that the more retirement fund options a person has, the less likely they are to save for their old age.

- Sheena Iyengar

After your home and your business, your superannuation account will most likely be the next biggest asset you own. Make sure you understand how superannuation works and use it for your benefit. Over my years working as an accountant and financial planner, I find most people don't take their superannuation account balances seriously. Around 1.8 million people in Australia rely solely on the age pension for their income in retirement because they did not save enough during their working years. Unfortunately, when some clients have retired, if their superannuation balance is small and below $100,000, they either withdraw the money to pay off their home loan or have a holiday and do not think of the long-term impact this will have on their retirement.

As at September 2018 if you qualify for the full age pension your entitlement is $916.30 per fortnight (or $23,824 p.a.) for singles and $690.70 each per fortnight for couples (or $35,916 p.a.).

Understanding Superannuation

Superannuation is nothing more than an investment savings vehicle with special rules. I personally believe in Australia we have one of the best retirement savings schemes in the world. We have so much freedom of choice as to which super fund we can use (e.g. industry super fund, public offer fund or even a self-managed superannuation fund) and control over how our moneys are invested and when we can have access to it (no one makes you take a pension out of the fund when you reach age 65). There are huge tax advantages in superannuation which most people do not fully understand or appreciate.

When money is contributed into superannuation and you or the business has claimed a tax deduction, then 15% tax will be deducted from the contribution by the super fund. This is called a concessional contribution. Whilst you are working and contributing to super your superannuation money is in the accumulation phase. Whilst your account is in accumulation, each year the earnings in the superannuation fund e.g. the interest income, dividends, rent or trust distribution, will only pay a tax rate of 15%. If you compare this to having the money invested in your personal name, the tax rate you would pay on the earnings could be 32.5%, 37% or even 45% plus 2% for Medicare.

Another significant advantage is if your superannuation fund sells an asset or investment and it has been owned by the fund for at least 12 months before it is sold, you will only pay 10% tax on any capital gains made on that sale.

When you retire and start a pension from your super fund, the great news is that if your account balance is below the current $1.6 million threshold, then you will pay NO tax on the income or capital gain earned in the super fund. For example, if you own an investment property in your superannuation fund, and the rent each year is $30,000, you will receive this income tax free - and if you then sell the property and make a capital gain of $100,000 then no tax is payable on that gain.

In the future as your superannuation account balance grows, you may then want to consider using a self-managed superannuation fund (SMSF). For many small business owners using a SMSF (and borrowing in super if necessary) to buy their business premises can be exciting and financially rewarding. I will focus on self-managed superannuation funds in the next chapter.

Contributions into Superannuation

There are two types of contributions you can make.

a) A concessional contribution up to $25,000 each year. This can either be from your employer or you personally.

b) A non-concessional contribution of up to $100,000 can be made each year, provided your account balance in super is below $1.5 million. You also can take advantage of the "bring forward" rules if your superannuation balance is below $1.3 million. You can then contribute up to $300,000 to super in one year.

But if you make the $300,000 contribution, for the following two financial years, you cannot contribute any further non-concessional contributions to super. It is important you work with an accountant or financial planner and understand each year what the superannuation contribution limits are and if you qualify to use them.

The rules for superannuation keep changing and the strategies you can use to contribute to superannuation are numerous. Below is a brief summary of some the main strategies to use with your superannuation fund. Talk to a financial planner and see if you can utilise some of these strategies in the future to obtain a tax deduction or benefit.

a) Co – contribution - If you are a low or middle-income earner and make personal (after-tax) contributions to your super fund up to $1,000, the government will also contribute (called a co-contribution) to your super fund up to a maximum amount of $500. You need to check the thresholds to see if you can take advantage of this.

b) Spouse contribution - To improve the superannuation balances of low-income spouses (their income is below $37,000), the government allows you to contribute up to $3,000 into your spouse's super account. By contributing the $3,000 you will qualify in your personal tax return for a $540 tax offset.

c) Downsizer contribution - From 1 July 2018, individuals 65 years old or older may be eligible to make a downsizer contribution into their superannuation of up to $300,000 from the proceeds of selling their home. This is a great way to boost your retirement savings in superannuation and take advantage of the low rates of tax on these investment earnings.

d) Carry-forward contribution - From 1 July 2018, you will now be able to make "carry-forward" concessional super contributions if your total superannuation balance is less than $500,000. The first year in which this strategy can be used is in the 2019–20 financial year. You will be able to access any unused concessional contributions cap space on a rolling basis for the previous five years. Amounts carried forward that have not been used after five years will expire.

For example, in the 2018/2019 financial year you only claimed $10,000 (out of the potential $25,000 you were entitled to contribute and claim) as a concessional contribution. In the following 2019/2020 year if you sell an asset or your business makes a significant profit, to help reduce the tax, you are entitled to contribute the annual limit of $25,000 to super and also contribute the $15,000 you did not use from the previous financial year. You will now be able to claim a $40,000 superannuation contribution as a tax deduction in one year.

This is a great initiative and I can see many small business owners taking advantage of this in future years.

How Much Super Do I Need?

How comfortable will your retirement be if you have no other savings or reserves to supplement the age pension? What do you envisage doing in your retirement? Travelling around Australia or overseas? Going camping or enjoying hobbies like golf or tennis? How will you pay for these dreams and will you be able to afford it?

A question I am often asked is how much money is needed in superannuation for a comfortable retirement. For a couple it is estimated under the Association of Superannuation Funds of Australia (ASFA) retirement standard (based on December 2018 figures) that an annual income of $60,977 will provide a couple with a comfortable retirement. To achieve this amount, a couple should have accumulated in superannuation a lump sum of $640,000. If you are a single person, it's estimated you will need to have saved $545,000 to ensure you have a comfortable retirement with an annual income of $43,317.

ASFA Retirement Standard	Annual living costs	Weekly living costs
Couple - modest	$39,775	$762
Couple - comfortable	$60,977	$1,168
Single - modest	$27,648	$530
Single - comfortable	$43,317	$830

These are just an estimate as no one knows how long you will live and what lifestyle you want in your retirement. I have clients who are comfortable on $60,000 p.a. whilst others require $150,000 p.a. to live on. Obviously, each person's needs and lifestyle requirements are different and therefore they will require a different lump sum amount to accumulate by the time they retire. With the improvement in medical research and health advice, people are enjoying a better quality of life and living longer, and it is estimated many will live to 85-90 years of age. The one fear most of my clients have when they retire is that they will outlive their money, which we call longevity risk.

At my seminars, clients regularly tell me, "My business is my superannuation. I am re-investing everything into the business and making it grow". In theory this sounds great, but over the years several of my clients have either been unable to find a purchaser for their business or if they do find a purchaser, they do not receive the sale price they were expecting.

If you are able to sell your business, this will be a bonus to your retirement nest egg. Rather than relying on the potential sale of your business, I recommend taking control of your future retirement plans.

Using superannuation to build your retirement savings is easy. Contributing regularly to superannuation each year and taking advantage of the reduced tax rates on investments held in superannuation, will help provide you with a more comfortable retirement in the future.

Most people in business underestimate the benefits superannuation provides as an asset protection tool. If you are in a profession or business where you may be sued, or made bankrupt, the moneys held in your superannuation fund are generally protected from the creditors or liquidators.

The added benefit of superannuation that is often overlooked but is incredibly powerful is compound interest. Albert Einstein called it the "Eighth Wonder of the World". The benefit of compounding interest works wonderfully in superannuation by the simple fact you cannot touch this money and it is invested until your retirement, which for most people will be age 60. By contributing amounts regularly each year into superannuation, and with the earnings also being reinvested each year, you get the multiplier benefit of additional interest being earned on those reinvested earnings.

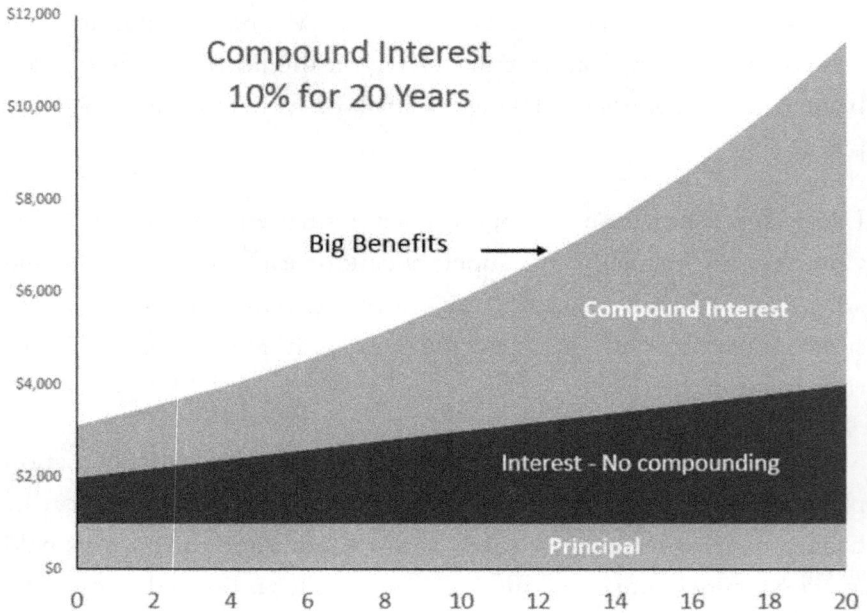

Compound Interest
10% for 20 Years

Many small business owners struggle to find the money to pay superannuation for themselves. There are always other expenses which are a priority like the rent, their suppliers, loan repayments, etc.

That is why in my earlier chapters I stress the importance of knowing your numbers and understanding your cash flow. It is time you take control of your finances and pay yourself first. It is important that you start saving regularly and make yourself a priority. As a minimum I advise my clients to be paying themselves superannuation of 9.5% of the weekly wage or drawings they take out of the business bank account to live on.

You would never work for another employer who did not pay superannuation for you, so why do you treat yourself any differently to any other employee in your firm?

I suggest clients initially start a regular savings plan by paying a small amount into superannuation each week or month. It might start with $50 or $100 a week or $500 a month, whatever amount you can afford now.

The next step in the process is in April or May prior to the end of the financial year do your tax planning with your tax accountant or financial planner. If you have a tax bill looming for this financial year and provided your cash flow allows, consider making a top up contribution to your super up to the maximum allowable concessional contribution which currently is $25,000 p.a. (as at 1 July 2018). You will achieve two things - firstly, you will reduce the amount of tax you have to pay, and secondly you will be providing for your retirement.

For example, if you have been paying $100 per week to super – you will have contributed by the end of April $4,400 to superannuation (44 weeks x $100). If you have the money you would be allowed to make a further contribution to superannuation of $20,600 ($25,000 less $4,400). By contributing the total amount of $20,600 into super and assuming your personal tax rate is 32.5% you will then have saved yourself tax of $6,695. At the same time, you now have increased your super account balance by $21,250. ($25,000 less 15% contributions tax deducted by the fund).

Even if you can't afford to contribute $20,600 just contribute $5,000 or whatever amount you can – it will all make a difference in saving tax and saving for your retirement. By doing this consistently over five, 10 and 20 years you will then see the savings grow and multiply.

For example, your business which is operating in a family trust has currently made a profit for this financial year of $110,000. As discussed above you have already contributed to superannuation $4,400. After meeting with your accountant, you have decided you can afford to make another $10,000 contribution to superannuation. It is assumed all the income will be distributed to you for this financial year. We have also done the comparison as if you could make the $20,600 contribution.

Personal Taxation:

Item	No Strategy	Strategy 1	Strategy 2
Trust Income	$110,000	$110,000	$110,000
Less Deductible Expenses:			
Superannuation contributions to date	$4,400	$4,400	$4,400
Additional superannuation contributions	$Nil	$10,000	$20,600
Taxable Income	$105,600	$95,600	$85,000
Tax on Taxable Income	$30,136	$23,004	$19,172

*Ignore Medicare Levy

Superannuation Fund Taxation:

Accumulation Fund	No Strategy	Strategy 1	Strategy 2
Taxable Contributions	$4,400	$14,400	$25,000
Tax on Contributions 15%	$660	$2,160	$3,750

Total Taxation Summary:

Item	No Strategy	Strategy 1	Strategy 2
Personal Taxation	$30,136	$23,004	$19,172
Superannuation Taxation	$660	$2,160	$3,750
Total Taxation	$30,796	$25,164	$22,922
Net Extra Tax Savings		$5,632	$7,874

If you can afford to do an extra $10,000 contribution to superannuation you will save an additional $5,632 in tax for that year. Should you be able to find an additional $20,600 to contribute to superannuation so you contribute the maximum of $25,000 then you will save $7,874 in that year.

Review Your Super Statement

It is important you review your annual superannuation statements. As your superannuation balance increases, you may find that the fund you currently use is no longer suitable or appropriate for your circumstances. Generally, if your account balance is below $100,000 you should only require an industry superannuation fund where the fees are low and the investment options are sufficient for this sum of money. The exception to this would be if you require insurance and it is held in super, then rather than owning several policies it may be efficient and cost-effective to only hold one policy.

As a minimum you should annually review your superannuation statement for the following:

- How is your super invested, and what is the asset allocation for the moneys held in your superannuation fund? What percentage is held in cash, fixed interest, Australian shares, international shares and property? You want to make sure your portfolio is diversified and invested across the different asset classes.

- What is your risk profile -how much do you expect to earn on those funds and how much are you prepared to lose? Can you sleep at night if your portfolio is too volatile and drops by 10% in value? Most people want a high rate of return but little or no volatility on the portfolio.

- What other investment options are available? Should you change or keep the option you have?

- Are you paying for insurance in this policy? If yes, do you need those insurances or are there other insurance options available which are cheaper or better?

- What fees and charges are you being charged on your superannuation policy? It is important you monitor these as they can easily erode your account balance and therefore your retirement savings.

If you have more than one superannuation policy, then it is time to review them and decide if you should consolidate/roll them over to just one super fund. Prior to doing this, seek advice from a financial planner before you consolidate your super funds. I recently met with a client who had rolled over all six super funds into one account, but in the process had cancelled over $300,000 of life insurance cover and now his family are exposed as he has no other insurance cover.

If over your working life, you have changed jobs, moved to a new house or worked in different industries you may have other super policies you have forgotten about. You should do a lost super search. Most super funds will provide this service for free or alternatively log onto the myGov website to track your lost super.

Your three action steps for this chapter are:

1. Review your annual super statement/s. Check how the fund is invested and what fees are being charged. If there are any insurances on the policy, do you need them and/or are they adequate for your occupation?

   As you review your superannuation funds, before consolidating them if you have several funds, get advice from a financial planner to make sure you do not lose any benefits.

2. Review how much you are currently contributing to super. If you are not currently paying yourself any super, then as a minimum pay weekly/monthly 9.5% into super of the amount of wages or drawings you are withdrawing from the business. Start with $100 a week and increase this as your cash flow in the business improves.

3. In April or May each year, do some tax planning with your accountant or financial planner so you can then decide if you should make a top up contribution to the maximum allowable concessional contribution of $25,000 prior to 30 June or utilise some of the other superannuation savings strategies allowed.

Chapter 7
Super on Steroids

Countries get one chance in history of putting into place a savings retirement scheme on the scale of the Australian superannuation system.

- Paul Keating

A self-managed superannuation fund (SMSF) is not suitable for everyone. Unless you want to buy direct property or do active share trading, there are cheaper superannuation options for you to consider.

Most people have heard about SMSFs but are not sure what is involved to set one up or how they work. The Australian Securities & Investment Commission (ASIC) and the ATO generally advise a minimum of $200,000 in super is required to establish a SMSF. That is one reason why I recommended clients contribute to super and build up their account balance in anticipation that in a couple of years' time, they will have saved enough to set up a SMSF.

The good news is a SMSF currently allows you to have a maximum of four members in the one fund. The government recently proposed in the 2018 May Budget increasing this to six members.

A SMSF is normally suited to family members (e.g. you and your spouse) or close business partners, who by combining up to four individual superannuation balances into the one SMSF may now have sufficient funds to purchase a property or use the funds as a deposit for the property purchase.

The purchase of business premises is not the only reason you would set up a SMSF, but it will be the focus of this chapter. I want you to see the wow factor and how superannuation really shines in helping you save for your retirement and increase your savings.

For example, if the business is a company and it pays rent to the SMSF for the property it uses, it will obtain a tax deduction and save tax at the 27.5% tax rate. The superannuation fund will only pay tax on this rental income at a maximum 15% or even better 0% tax rate if the fund is in pension mode. This will provide an annual tax saving of 12.5% overall for your group of entities.

Setting Up a SMSF

The legal cost to set up a SMSF can vary from NIL (by internet providers who then have you commit to do the accounting work with them) up to $2,500. I recommend speaking to an accredited financial planner or accountant to initially discuss if a SMSF is suitable for you. You need to determine who will be a member, how much do they each already have in superannuation and will a SMSF really be the best structure for you to use for this property purchase transaction.

At times I will recommend clients wait another 12 to 18 months until the balance in their superannuation fund has increased before setting up a SMSF. The best investment you can make is to pay for advice prior to setting up a SMSF and rolling over your money. There are additional costs involved in owning a property in a SMSF which sometimes clients have not been made aware of. I have at times advised clients to not proceed with a property purchase where based on my research:

a) it was not viable for the SMSF to purchase the property at that purchase price; or

b) if they still want to purchase the property, to not purchase it in a SMSF but to use a family trust or purchase it in their own name.

Years later I have had clients return to thank me for stopping them from purchasing the property, which now thanks to hindsight, would have been a big mistake. I was able to take the emotion and heat out of the transaction and help them minimise the potential financial damage to their retirement savings.

A SMSF is designed to give people more control and choice over their retirement savings and investment options. But people often underestimate the time needed to run and maintain a SMSF as well as the money required to operate it.

The annual costs of operating a SMSF are often overlooked in the calculations when deciding if owning a property in a SMSF is viable or not. In addition to the annual financial statements and tax return being prepared, your super fund will need to be audited. As a minimum, you can expect to pay between $1,500 to $3,000 p.a. in annual administration costs. This is in addition to the normal costs of investing in and owning a rental property (e.g. rates, body corporate fees, insurance) or managing a share or managed funds investment portfolio.

Having a SMSF means that all members need to be a trustee of the SMSF or a director of the trustee company. You are assumed to be actively involved in making decisions about your investments and interests in the SMSF. There have been recent court cases where a trustee of a SMSF has been jailed or fined for the illegal actions of one of the other trustees.

Immediately upon establishing a SMSF you are required to sign a trustee declaration which explains what your duties and obligations are as a trustee. The courts will not accept the line of defence, "My husband looked after everything and I never read the minutes or understood the financial statements and just signed where I was told to sign".

If you are going to spend the money to set up a SMSF from my experience having a corporate trustee is preferable to individual trustees. The trustee company will provide you with asset protection, especially if you are buying a commercial or residential property, and some estate planning benefits.

One of the main estate planning benefits of having a corporate trustee can be utilised if a member should lose capacity. The attorney appointed under the enduring power of attorney (EPOA) for the person who has lost capacity can step in as a director of the corporate trustee and continue to operate the SMSF on behalf of the member. If a member loses capacity and does not have an EPOA, technically they can no longer be a member of the SMSF, and their account balance must be rolled out of the fund. This could force the SMSF to have to sell assets, so it has the funds to roll out that member's account balance. To avoid this happening, all members of a SMSF should have a valid enduring power of attorney.

As soon as a SMSF is established, an investment strategy should be prepared for the fund where all the trustees decide what investments the SMSF will want to buy and own. This document should be reviewed annually and monitored, to ensure the funds in the super fund are invested in accordance with the investment strategy. It is important that all members are involved in selecting the investments, not just one member controlling and making all the decisions about the fund.

If you have not quite accumulated the $200,000 needed to set up the SMSF or do not have the required amount to buy the property, then do not establish it yet as you will pay unnecessary accounting and audit fees for each year the money is only sitting in a term deposit or bank account. Numerous times, clients unwisely establish the SMSF too early and end up frustrated their retirement savings are eroded by having to pay for the annual audit and financial statements to be prepared.

Buying Property in a SMSF

As previously mentioned, most of my clients use a SMSF for the benefit of purchasing their business premises. There are several ways you can structure the purchase of the property.

a) Buy it outright. If you have accumulated sufficient funds in superannuation already or maybe you have funds held in your personal name which you can contribute to super to build up your account balance to enable you to purchase the property outright.

In Chapter 6, we discussed making concessional contributions of $25,000 per person, non-concessional contributions of $100,000 each or using the three year "bring forward" rule for contributions up to $300,000 each to accumulate enough funds to be able to buy the property in the SMSF.

For example, Allan and Fay have a total of $220,000 in two industry super funds. They have found a warehouse to buy which will cost $400,000. Ignoring the added costs of stamp duty and legal fees at this stage, they have a shortfall of $180,000. Allan recently received an inheritance from Aunt Mavis of $250,000 and was wondering what to do with this money. By making a non-concessional contribution of $250,000 into the SMSF there will now be enough cash for them to buy the property without needing a loan from the bank.

b) In specie contribution into a SMSF. This option MAY be available to someone who already owns business real property in their personal name and wants to contribute it to their SMSF so the property will have asset protection, they can save tax and increase their retirement savings. Please talk to your professional advisors before considering this option to see if it is viable for you to make the non-concessional contribution and pay the stamp duty costs. If the transaction will trigger a potential capital gains tax bill in your name it may not be advisable proceeding with the transaction.

c) Should a client not have enough funds in a self-managed super fund, then they can consider implementing what's called a limited recourse borrowing arrangement (LRBA) which allows them to borrow the shortfall to be able to buy the property.

Limited Recourse Borrowing Arrangement (LRBA)

Purchasing a property in a SMSF using a LRBA requires the SMSF to set up a bare trust and another trustee company. The arrangement needs to be structured in a similar way to the diagram below.

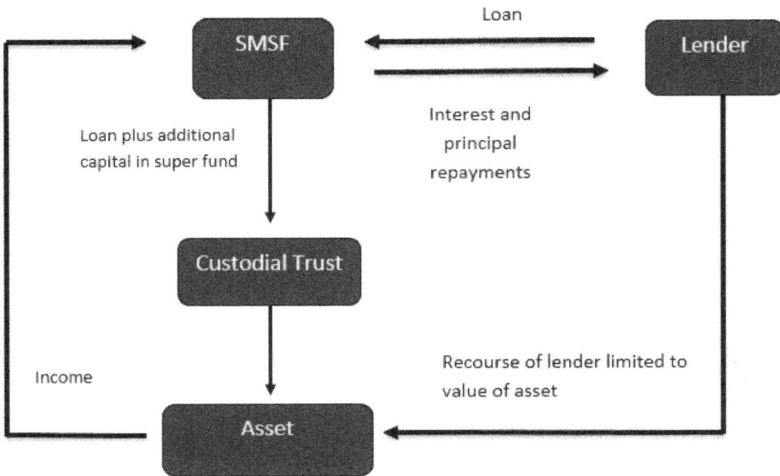

Below is an example of the costs a client may incur if they wish to purchase their business premises valued at $600,000. The real cost of acquiring the property is estimated as follows:

Purchase details	Amount
Purchase price	$600,000
Purchase costs (inclusive of Stamp duty, set up costs)	
Stamp duty & transfer fee (Queensland)	$21,869
Legal Fees for purchase of property & lease	$4,000
Bank Loan set up costs, valuations	$10,000
Set up SMSF, bare trust and trustee companies	$4,400
Financial planning advice fees	$5,500
Total cost	**$645,769**

The client only had $250,000 in their two superannuation funds so the only way they would be able to buy the property would be if they could borrow within a SMSF. The banks will currently lend up to 60-70% of the commercial property value.

Based on the valuation of $600,000, the SMSF will be able to borrow $420,000 and the SMSF will need to provide $225,769 to make the purchase happen.

Loan Required	Amount
Total cost of purchase	$645,769
Loan – 70% of property value x $600,000	$420,000
Shortfall of funds required in SMSF	$225,769

A couple of important things to highlight:

i) While the purchase price of the property is $600,000, when you add the additional fees and charges payable the true cost of purchasing the property is $645,769. The costs will vary from state to state, especially with stamp duty and legal fees and if you already have a SMSF set up.

ii) Allow extra time in the contract for settlement for the SMSF and bare trust to be established and to apply for an ABN. You then need to allow time to organise the rollovers of the existing superannuation funds into the SMSF. Also discuss with your bank how long they will need to approve the loan and settle – these transactions usually take longer than a normal home loan purchase.

iii)   Every state has different rules about which name is to be listed on the contract of sale as the purchaser. Please check with your legal advisers as you may otherwise incur additional stamp duty costs.

iv)   Following the Royal Commission into the banking sector in 2018, many of the major banks in Australia have stopped lending to SMSFs. The government has not indicated it will be stopping LRBAs in the future. I feel the major banks are under the spotlight for so many other banking issues this is one headache and complication they do not need at this time. However, there are still several smaller financial institutions willing to lend money to SMSFs.

v)   The business must be able to pay the commercial rent on the property and continue to make annual contributions to super for you. This will then ensure you can afford to make the loan repayments each month. When you do your calculations, you need to also factor if the SMSF will be able to pay the loan repayments should interest rates rise in the future by 2% during the term of the loan.

The benefits of doing a limited recourse borrowing arrangement are numerous. You can rent the premises to your business, have flexibility restructuring the lease, the outgoings are reimbursed by the business to the super fund and you control where your business operates from without fear of being evicted from your premises in the future.

Assuming you hold onto the property for 10 to 15 years, it will hopefully have increased in value. A significant benefit of holding property in a SMSF is the reduced capital gains tax you will pay compared to if you held the property in your personal name or a company. If you are in accumulation phase you will only pay 10% tax on the gain and if you are retired and receiving a pension, then 0% tax on the gain.

Using the example earlier, we paid $600,000 for the property and 15 years later we sell the property for $720,000. There is a capital gain of $120,000 and the tax payable in the SMSF at 10% will be $12,000. If you wait till you are retired and in pension mode, then no capital gains tax would be payable at all.

Sale of property	SMSF – Accumulation 10% tax	SMSF – Pension 0% tax	Investment in Personal Name *
Sale Price	$720,000	$720,000	$720,000
Less Purchase Price	$600,000	$600,000	$600,000
Capital Gain	$120,000	$120,000	$120,000
Assessable Capital Gain	$120,000	$120,000	$60,000
Net Tax Payable	$18,000	$Nil	$11,617

*Assuming no other income in personal name or Medicare Levy

Subsequent Years - Property in a SMSF

You now have made it into year two or three of owning a SMSF. Things should have settled down with the expenses and loan repayments. You begin to realise the time involved in managing the compliance for your SMSF and in managing the investments. You are managing a separate legal entity and you need to keep copies of all invoices for each expense and income transaction in your SMSF, especially as this entity will be audited. The responsibility for ensuring the fund is complying will rest with you as the trustee as you signed the trustee declaration to undertake this responsibility.

It is important that you understand your responsibilities as to which investments you can buy in a self-managed super fund. A common mistake I see is where clients want to buy residential property in their SMSF and rent it to their parents or children. You can own a residential investment property in a SMSF, but you cannot rent it to your relatives. The only investment you can buy and use yourself is business real property where you can buy your business premises or factory and rent that to your business.

I am constantly asked about doing boutique investments like bitcoin or even gold or coins. If you are interested in purchasing these types of investment seek advice to make sure the paperwork is compliant and will pass the audit.

In subsequent years as the business continues to grow and pays the SMSF rent, every three years you will need a market valuation to advise you how much rent should be paid. When the lease is due for renewal, it is the ideal time to review it and make amendments like including the outgoings such as rates, body corporate fees and insurance to now be paid by the business. This will increase the tax deductions in the business reducing the profit and tax payable by the business whilst at the same time allowing your retirement savings to increase.

For example:

	Company (Tax rate 27.5%)	SMSF (Tax Rate 15%)
Expenses (excluding rent)		
Rates	$5,000	$5,000
Body Corp	$4,000	$4,000
Insurance	$7,000	$7,000
Total (a)	$16,000	$16,000
Tax saved at the applicable tax rate on the total expenses x (a)	$4,400 (b)	$2,400 (c)
Extra tax saved each year (b) – (c)	$2,000	

Final Note on SMSFs

By now you would have realised that setting up, owning and operating a SMSF is complicated and you need to get it right the first time. I especially recommend you work with professional advisors in the first few years as you become familiar with the rules and legal requirements of owning a SMSF. I assist clients with setting up their SMSF and purchasing their property and we then work with their accountants who prepare the annual financial statements and audit. Each year monitor the progress of the SMSF and check it is in accordance with the investment strategy.

At the end of the day, you as the member and trustee of the super fund will be responsible for the decisions that are made and the paperwork you have signed. It will be great to think you can blame the accountant or the investment advisor, but ultimately you as a member and trustee of the SMSF will be who the ATO will be holding accountable.

Your three action steps for this chapter are:

1. If you are interested in having your own self-managed super fund, spend time to educate yourself. The ATO has great resources on their website for you to download and read. Attend seminars in your local area but be aware of the property spruikers. Their only aim is to convince you to buy one of their properties and often off the plan.

   I regularly hold seminars on SMSFs covering different topics like setting up a SMSF, buying a property in a SMSF and retirement planning.

2. If you have found a property you think you would like to buy in a SMSF, prior to signing a contract, meet with an accountant or financial planner. Review your existing super balances and determine if it is worthwhile to set up a SMSF and if you will be able to rollover your existing super fund balances. Ensure you first check you are not cancelling any insurances or jeopardising any other features or benefits that may exist in your current super fund.

3. If you are considering buying a property using a limited recourse borrowing arrangement (LRBA), do your research early before your find the property. How much do you want to spend on purchasing a property and do you have enough in superannuation, or do you need to increase your superannuation balance/s prior to setting up a SMSF or signing a contract to purchase a property? Know if you will be able to afford the property and be able to meet the loan repayments. There may be other options to consider in purchasing the property without using a SMSF and/or LRBA.

Chapter 8
It's Getting Real

I am very concerned about the millions of baby boomers who are counting on the stock market to deliver them a safe, sound, long retirement. I am afraid the baby boomers who are counting on the stock market are in trouble.

- Robert Kiyosaki

Five years prior to retirement is the perfect time to review how you are tracking with the goals you set yourself in previous years. Now is also the ideal time to plan for the future and identify if you need to make any changes to achieve your goals for retirement. If you are not on target, you still have time to make changes and influence the outcome. If you spend the time now and in each subsequent year, reviewing your numbers can make a huge difference to your successful retirement.

This chapter will focus on two main areas:

1. Getting your business ready for sale in five years' time; and

2. Are you achieving your goals and milestones?

Getting Your Business Ready for Sale

The reality is that selling a business is hard work, but it can be so financially rewarding if it is done right. You need to invest time on your business to prepare it for sale. This may mean restructuring your business so that it is a smooth transition for the new owner to operate. It should be presented in the best light so that you can maximise your sale price and the buyer can see themselves succeeding in the business.

Ninety percent of business owners believe they are not prepared for "the sale" when they finally go to sell their business. The average sale price most small business owners achieve for all those years of hard work is only 1.5 times the **PROFIT.** We were fortunate when selling our accounting practice in the year 1999/2000, to be paid dollar for dollar on the **TURNOVER** amount, not the profit. We were able to achieve this because the accounting business had regular and loyal clients who came back year after year to have their tax returns prepared. Yes, this was back in 2000 and maybe in 2019 we would not achieve the same sale price.

When trying to sell your business, you will need to be cognisant of the industry you are in. For instance, the financial planning industry currently is in turmoil due to the recent Royal Commission and changes to the education standard requirements expected in the near future for all financial planners. What we can already see is there will be a major exodus from the financial planning industry over the next few years and their business valuations in the next five years will diminish significantly. You need to take steps now to reduce the impact of any possible decline in your business value if you can see a potential threat to its value in the future.

In the past few years I have seen several medical general practitioner doctors who even with a regular, loyal patient database have been unable to sell their business, especially since the big corporate medical practices have come into their towns and cities. These big medical practices just wait for the older GPs to retire and when people next urgently seek medical advice, by default they take over their client list.

Some other GPs had the foresight four to five years earlier to sponsor an overseas doctor or to bring a younger doctor into the business with the aim of implementing a succession plan. They planned for this early enough, so they could sell the business and gradually retire providing a smooth transition to the new owner.

Also, with some planning ahead you may be able to minimise the tax you will pay when you do sell the business. This is a critical time to start talking to your accountant or financial planner and advising them of your vision and plans.

Five years prior to retirement may be the ideal time for small business owners to think about succession planning. A succession plan is a long-term event that may take months and in some cases years to implement. It is important as a small business owner to think about any potential people who may want to purchase or take over the business. This usually works successfully where you have a child, family member or an employee who has been working in the business who may wish to take it over in the future.

Some small business owners incorrectly assume their children will want to step up when they retire and take over the business. Unfortunately, the reality is the children are happy working in the business and receiving a good wage, but do not necessarily want the actual responsibility of running a business in the future.

Fortunately, I have also worked with other business owners where one or two of their children have happily transitioned to take over the business over a period of a couple of years and have then grown the business to the next level successfully.

To avoid family disagreements in the future, if you have other children who will not be working in the business, it is important you document and formalise a sale agreement and document the valuation you will use in selling the business and how the transaction will be structured. For example, the price may be paid off in instalments like vendor finance over a five-year period or you may do a partial sale of shares to your child of 15% or 20% interest in the business each year.

In the lead up to a sale of the business, you may need to check what qualifications, accreditations or registrations the person will require to be able to take over your business. Your potential candidate may need to undertake some additional training or obtain certain accreditations to be able to operate the business, e.g. liquor licence if they are operating a restaurant or night club or a gold card for the construction industry.

It may take time to groom a suitable candidate to take over your business. If your children are not interested or you do not have children, then maybe you can consider grooming an employee or two who may be interested. Sometimes just planting the seed in their mind and showing them a future career path may be all it takes to find a future purchaser of your business. Starting five years earlier will allow them time to save enough money for the purchase or consider options for structuring the transaction.

Alternatively, you may need to look external to the business and employ someone new, with the offer they will become a business partner over the next few years until they eventually end up with 100% control.

Working as an employee in the business is completely different to running it and does require a different mindset. Your employee may never have even considered buying a business or being able to afford it – but you are now presenting them with a fantastic opportunity and showing them a pathway as to how this can be achieved.

Legalities to Consider

During the period you are negotiating the succession plan it is important that both parties are honest and evaluate how the process is working and if the buyer still wants to take over the business when you are ready to retire.

It is also a good time to ensure a confidentiality agreement and any succession planning documents are signed. This may also be the right time to introduce some form of profit share or incentive to ensure you commit the employee or candidate to the business and they do not just walk away and set up a business next door and take all your ideas, research, systems and processes. The succession plan is a written plan that can be followed and will show the milestones so each party can check in and evaluate whether you keep progressing the sale of the business.

Partial ownership may also be an option to consider. You may start transferring 10% of the business at a time over three to four years, so gradually that person has now acquired 30-40% of the business. Obviously, another consideration is the remuneration package and wage you are currently paying this person and is it at an appropriate level or not, when you consider as well any profit share or distribution they may receive. If you are operating in a family trust this might be the time to transition the business to a private company structure.

The next few years will be the ideal time for you to start stepping out of the business and maybe reduce your working hours. If you have spent the time putting systems and procedures in place, you may only need to work a three or four day working week, or alternatively you may have competent managers operating the business so that you are comfortable leaving them in charge while you go overseas and take a two or three month break from the business. This is actually a great test to see if the business can operate without you or at least if you can work remotely. In these days of cloud-based accounting and being connected on the Internet, staying in touch and monitoring the business is much easier than it has ever been.

It is important you consider all the potential purchasers for your business and what will work for you. You need to think about when you will retire and whether the transition will happen over a few years or a shorter period of time. This will be something your accountant and lawyers will be able to explore in more detail as well as looking at any alternative legal structures or options for you to make the business sale a success.

Review Your Goals and Milestones

In my experience many business owners wait till they reach age 60 (or whatever age they thought they would retire) and then start to plan for their retirement. They suddenly realise they have not saved enough money and now need to continue to work for a couple more years. How many times do you reflect back on the past year and wonder where did the last 12 months go – that year just flew by. It will sneak up on you and often the reality hits when your friends and business associates start to retire, and you may then realise the inadequate state of your own financial position.

Making the time five years prior to your intended retirement date to review your goals and determine if you are on track allows you the time and opportunity to make changes so you can still achieve your dreams and goals.

Based on what your thoughts are for selling or growing your business as determined in the earlier section of this chapter, you should now be able to make a plan for your personal goals too.

If you cannot find the time to review your goals and see how you are tracking in achieving these goals, you will miss the opportunity to make any changes to your budget or business processes which may actually be costing you money. If your turnover is not increasing year on year, what do you need to change or do differently to improve your financial position?

As discussed in Chapter 2, ensure your goals are written down and written in the present tense as if you have already achieved them. Also do not forget to use the SMART system when setting your goals. SMART stands for:

S – Specific

M - Measurable

A – Attainable (or Action-Oriented)

R – Relevant (or Rewarding)

T – Time Bound (or Trackable)

It is okay if your goals have changed over time and some things are now no longer a priority like they were five years or even one year earlier.

Clients will frequently say they do not have the time to do this as they are so busy working IN the business. If you want to retire financially secure, you need to make this a priority. You need to spend time working ON the business and not just IN your business.

As discussed earlier, looking forward will allow you to predict the direction your industry may be headed and if needed make any necessary changes to stay in front. For example, the growth in Airbnb may affect small motel operators, Uber Eats may affect the local takeaway shop in the suburbs, a sudden ban on live cattle exports will affect the whole rural industry and businesses associated with them - and do not forget the demise of the video/DVD shop.

Other Things to Consider

This is also a great time for you to start reviewing your expenses and your cash flow and check how you're tracking with your turnover, profit and wages, and any of the other goals you set yourself, so you can retire when you want.

Review your branding and marketing for the business as this might be the time for you to ramp up the business profile and increase your marketing activity. This should hopefully increase your sales with the ultimate aim of increasing the bottom line and your sale price.

Don't underestimate the benefits of reviewing and updating your systems and procedures regularly and ensuring you have checklists and systems in place for all departments in the business. The more you can document and remove yourself as the individual necessary to run the business and ensure the business operates independently without you, the better the sale price you will be able to achieve.

If you are in a business where when you retire, nobody will buy the business, then how are you going with building your retirement savings? Often personal service providers like jewellers, lawyers and doctors in general practice are unable to sell their businesses. Are you contributing the maximum to superannuation and are you doing everything you can to minimise tax and save money? It is far more critical for you to be regularly reviewing your budget and cash flow and saving for your retirement as there will not be any golden handshake or nest egg when you retire or try to sell the business. It's up to you and no one else to provide for your retirement. It's a great time now to review how your superannuation is performing as discussed in Chapter 6 and 7 and if necessary, change investment options or superannuation fund entirely.

If you are retiring at a younger age and unable to access your superannuation savings, you need to plan for an investment portfolio outside superannuation. For some people this may be owning a couple of investment properties and for others it may be a portfolio of managed funds/direct shares. You need to find out which investments will suit you and be able to pay you a steady income once you have retired and stopped work.

Your three action steps for this chapter are:

1. Review the goals you set for yourself five or 10 years earlier as discussed in Chapter 2. Are you achieving your annual goals for your business' profit, turnover target and wage you want paid from the business? Have you been able to save and contribute to superannuation?

2. Are you on target to retire the year/age you want and is the retirement income you want achievable?

   If not, what are you going to change now while you still have five years to make it happen? Everyone's goal is different. I have clients who want to retire at 60 and others will keep working to age 70. I have clients who only need an annual income of $50,000 to live on whilst others require $150,000. Obviously, the lump sum capital required at your retirement will be different depending on what your retirement goal is, the level of income you require and how many years you will not be working.

3. Make time to review the exit strategy/succession plan for your business and meet with your accountant and lawyer and determine what options will work for you. Do you need to restructure your business? Do you need to start grooming a family member, an existing employee or bring in a new employee with the aim in five years' time they will take over?

Chapter 9
Foolproof Exit Plan

Small business owners and entrepreneurs worthy of the title need to build systems that replace themselves.

- Michael E. Gerber

The time has finally arrived to sell your business. In the next five to 10 years there is going to be an increase in the number of businesses for sale as the baby boomers are now retiring. Currently 80% of small businesses are owned by baby boomers. If you have spent the time over the past five years getting your systems in order and procedures documented, you will be better placed to maximise the sale price you can achieve.

As the saying goes, "Turnover is vanity, profit is sanity and cash flow is king". When selling your business, the potential buyer will be looking at these three things and analysing what changes or improvements they can make to take it to another level. Business is valued on profit but is sold on the potential the new owner can achieve.

You want to be in control of choosing when you sell the business and not be forced to have to sell at an inappropriate time. You may be forced to sell your business due to ill health, a divorce, or falling out with a business partner.

Another event out of your control may arise if you are forced to relocate at the end of the lease or to undertake a refurbishment of the premises which is required by a clause in your lease. Either of these may be too expensive or unprofitable for the business to contemplate. Recently a well-known national franchise coffee shop in a major shopping centre was required as part of its lease agreement to undertake a complete refurbishment of the shop every five years. The business owners, when they reviewed their financials, could not justify spending the money to completely refurbish the premises and decided to cease operations when the lease expired.

If you have taken the time to set up the systems and procedures and the business is now operating independently of you this is what we call a turnkey operation. Potential purchasers of a business want to be able to walk into the business and be able to operate it without you from the next day. The potential purchaser of your business could even be an employee or two that may want to take over the business. Another option may be new migrants to Australia who within two years, as a condition of their visa, must purchase a business and establish themselves in the community.

Recently a business owner in Cairns was unable to find a buyer for the business. He approached two of his key employees to buy a half share each in the business. The business has continued to operate successfully.

If the turnover and profit in the business has been consistent over the past three to five years, the purchaser should then be able to access bank finance. You may need to consider offering vendor finance for part of the remaining balance.

Be realistic in your expectations of the sale price you can achieve. Some business owners believe after 20 to 30 years of blood, sweat and tears in the business, they should be rewarded. Unfortunately, if when the purchaser starts reviewing the profit and turnover of the business, these numbers do not justify the sale price you want, you will not find a buyer for the business.

Get advice and appoint a business broker who knows your industry, they will maximise the sale price and know how to market and position your business. You may need to do this one year prior to when you want to list the business for sale to make sure you can maximise your return.

When we sold the accounting business there was a requirement in the contract that I had to stay on for six months to ensure a smooth transition for the clients so they would not leave the firm. The purchaser of our business also had a clawback clause on the sale price in case the business turnover decreased by more than 20% in the first year. From the purchaser's perspective this meant minimal risk of the clients leaving the firm and if this did happen, he had mitigated his financial loss as we would have needed to reimburse him a portion of the sale proceeds.

I suggest you limit any handover period to no more than six months. Obviously, there will need to be a certain level of training and handing over, so you have time to introduce the purchaser to your customers, suppliers and contacts once the business is sold. It can be quite an emotional and testing time as you need to let go of your "baby" (your business). The new owner will have their own ideas they will want to introduce.

It is important to use a good commercial lawyer to prepare and review the conditions in the sale agreement. You do not want to be tied to the business or held responsible for things that are totally beyond your control. If you are providing vendor finance this needs to be in a separate agreement which is connected to the actual sale contract. It should include a clause for if the purchaser defaults at any time how you will be compensated. This will depend on the proportion of the sale price you financed but some business owners have been able to walk back in and take back the business when the purchaser defaulted and was unable to pay the negotiated price. We don't want to get to that stage, but it means you may then still have an asset to sell (again).

Capital Gains Tax

Before you list your business for sale you should talk to your accountant and consider the following questions:

a) Is this a good time to sell?

b) Is your business even ready to sell - are the systems, procedures and cash flow working well to maximise your sale price?

c) What do you need to do to minimise the capital gains tax on the sale?

This may be an ideal time to restructure the business or consider delaying the sale for another 12 to 18 months so you achieve 15 years of ownership and will be able to access additional capital gains tax concessions.

As a small business operator, you will most commonly make a capital gain or loss when you sell one of the assets used in your business, such as the business premises, or when you sell your business. We will only focus on these two scenarios in this chapter.

The good news is there are a number of CGT tax concessions which are only available to small business owners, so make sure you work with a good tax accountant who understands the CGT rules to ensure you minimise the tax you will pay on the sale of your business.

This book is not about giving you the specific tax advice or rules as they are so complicated and intricate. But I do want to highlight the importance of doing things in a certain order to qualify for the CGT concessions. Numerous times business owners come and see us AFTER the event when they have signed contracts or even completed the deal and then it is too late to take advantage of all the tax concessions they may have qualified for.

There is nothing more frustrating as a professional knowing we could have assisted a client to minimise the tax payable on the sale of their business or increased the amount of money contributed to their superannuation account.

To qualify for the small business concessions, you need to first satisfy either of the following tests:

a) Net Asset Value test – the net value of your assets needs to be less than $6 million. This is basically the value of all the assets you or your spouse own (excluding your home) and assets owned by the group of companies and trusts that you may control reduced by any loans or debts

b) Turnover test - this will be met if your business had turnover in the year you sell the asset of less than $2 million.

I recently worked with a client who owned a cattle property out west worth millions of dollars. They were advised in order to qualify under the $2 million turnover test, to wait until the following year when there was an expected downturn in cattle sales. If the client had not discussed this prior to the sale, she would have paid hundreds of thousands of dollars in capital gains tax.

There are potentially five small business concessions you may be eligible to use. These are the:

- **15-year exemption** - If your business has been in operation for more than 15 years then you qualify for 100% exemption on the capital gain and will pay NO TAX. Recently a dentist who had been in business for 18 years was able to sell his business for $1 million and contribute the entire sale proceeds of $1 million into his superannuation fund as it was below the allowable contribution threshold at that time of $1,480,000. With all the new restrictions and limits on contributing to superannuation this opens the door for small business owners to add up to a maximum $1,480,000 to their superannuation account and invest those moneys in this low tax environment.

- **50% general CGT discount** - If you are a sole trader, partner in a partnership, trust beneficiary or individual selling your shares in a company (or units in a unit trust) and the asset has been held for more than 12 months, you will be eligible to claim the 50% general CGT discount. This concession is available to everyone, not just small business owners. In this scenario you and your spouse may have owned an investment property which you have just sold for $650,000. You bought the property eight years ago and paid $300,000 at that time. The capital gain would be calculated as follows:

Sale Price	$650,000
Cost	$300,000
Capital Gain	$350,000
Apply CGT Discount x 50%	$175,000
Capital Gain assessable	$175,000

As you and your spouse owned the property jointly only half of this amount $87,500 will be included in each of your individual tax returns in the year you sold the property. If we assume a tax rate of 37% you each would have paid tax of $32,375 or a total of $64,750.

- **50% active asset reduction** - This concession allows you to reduce the capital gain arising from an active business asset by a further 50%. Talk to your accountant to determine if the asset you are selling qualifies as an "active asset". A capital gain made on the sale of a business premises will often be able to be reduced under this election. Using the above scenario as an example, but instead we assume it is a warehouse used by the business.

Capital Gain assessable per above	$175,000
Less 50% active asset reduction	$ 87,500
Assessable capital gain	$ 87,500

Again, as you and your spouse owned the property jointly only half of this amount - $43,750 will be included in each of your individual tax returns in the year you sold the business premises. You can start to see how significant the tax savings can be by now being taxed in a much lower tax bracket. If we assume a tax rate of 32.5% you each would have paid tax of $14,219 or a total of $28,438.

If the warehouse had been owned by a company, although the company does not qualify for the 50% general CGT discount, you would have paid 27.5% tax on the $175,000 which would have been $48,125.

- **CGT retirement exemption** - This concession can exempt a capital gain on a business asset, up to a lifetime limit of $500,000. When you choose this option, there is no requirement for you to actually retire or cease business.

Continuing with our example above, if you wanted to reduce the tax even further assuming you are under the age of 55 you each could have contributed the capital gain amount of $43,750 into superannuation making a total of $87,500. You will then not need to pay the combined tax bill of $28,438.

Whether you use this concession will depend on your age and how close you are to retirement. By contributing $87,500 to superannuation you potentially lose access to this money until you retire, compared to paying the tax of $23,438 and being able to use in your personal name the remaining $59,062. This is a decision only you can make. You also would need to consider if there still was a mortgage on the property which needed to be repaid.

When I sold my business, I was 30 years old and I made the decision back then to contribute my $80,000 capital gain to super as I knew I was about to stop work and have children and probably would not be able to contribute to super for the next five to 10 years. Was it a hard decision at that time? – Yes. Do I regret it now 20 years later? - No. The money has grown, and it allowed us to have the funds to buy a property in our SMSF much sooner than we expected.

- **CGT rollover exemption** - This concession allows you to defer the capital gain from the disposal of a business asset for a minimum of two years. If you can acquire a replacement asset or make a capital improvement to an existing asset, you can defer the capital gain until a change in your circumstances causes this gain to crystallise. Talk to your accountant to see if you can utilise this election to defer or minimise the CGT you could potentially pay. This election gives you time to think about what your next step will be - and the good news is, even if you then want to put the money in superannuation in two years' time you can still do that.

Hopefully by now you realise the importance of considering which tax structure to use when buying an asset or setting up the business, as the tax consequences can be quite significant as shown in the above examples.

Depending on your circumstances you can access one or several of these elections at the time of sale. I cannot stress enough the importance of getting good advice outlining how you can minimise any potential tax in the future on the sale of your business or the assets in the business.

Maximise Your Sale Price

Get your business ready for sale 12 to 18 months prior. Look at ways to increase your profit, review your products' selling prices or your charge out rates. Review your expenses and see what can be streamlined, e.g. is the advertising and marketing working? If you have job costing and quoting in your business, measure those quotes against the actual time taken to complete the work. Sometimes complacency can creep into a business that has been established and operating successfully. Now might be the time to see if you can improve the productivity and tighten the belt on a few expenses. As the buyer will want to see three years of trading results, the more consistent your sales and profit are year on year, then the better the sale price you will be able to achieve.

If the purchaser can see your client base has consistent, regular customers who keep returning, that also will potentially increase your sale price. Don't get emotional when selling. If you get a good offer and it's a fair and good price, take it. Don't get greedy. Too many times clients have passed up on an offer and wanted to wait another year or two. When they were ready to sell, either the Global Financial Crisis happened or now they could not find a buyer for their business as significant changes occurred to the industry and the sale price was diminished.

Get an honest appraisal and valuation of your business. If you are serious about selling, meet with an accountant and business broker and get your financials in order to maximise the sale. These things should be organised prior to even listing your business for sale so you look professional and it is obvious you are selling under your terms and conditions and not as a fire sale or under duress.

Another thing to remember is once the business is listed for sale, first impressions count. Don't just assume that a purchaser is only going to come to you via the business broker. They may do their own homework and send in one or two secret shoppers to test your business and see how it operates. Their first impression of your business needs to be consistent and impress them so they will want to buy your business.

Make sure your business premises are looking spick-and-span. It is not unusual that the gardens may need some maintenance, or the building needs a coat of paint to freshen it up and make it look modern and up to date.

In Australia, every state will have its own laws, regulations and requirements on the sale or purchase of a business, licensing and registration requirements with local councils and if any stamp duty will be payable. Your business broker should be able to provide you with this information.

Always ensure that before you release any financial information or intellectual property, the potential buyer has signed a confidentiality agreement. You also should do your own due diligence on the potential buyer and ensure they are genuine and they have the necessary qualifications and the finances to purchase the business.

Even if you go to contract, it is still normal for the purchaser's accountant to undertake a due diligence on your business and review your financials and customer list to see if your asking price is justified and warranted.

Appoint a good commercial lawyer at this time to ensure your business is protected from the potential misuse of your information by a purchaser who does not proceed.

I highly recommend if you have the time to read Sam Harrop's book, *Small Business, Big Exit*, which is about maximising the sale price for your business.

Your three action steps for this chapter are:

1. If you are now ready to sell your business talk to your accountant and discuss the time frame for when you wish to sell and have them provide you with an estimate of what would be a fair price for your business. Once you know the potential sale price, are you happy to accept this amount or what do you now need to do to improve things before you list the business for sale?

2. Talk to your business broker and get their advice on what needs to be done to list the business for sale and maximise your sale price. If you need financial statements, a formal

valuation or brochures prepared arrange these now. Do the business premises or garden need a tidy up?

3. Talk to your commercial lawyer to ensure confidentiality agreements are prepared prior to listing the business for sale. Don't just rely on the documents your business broker may provide you – have your lawyer review them to ensure they are robust enough for your industry and business. Have your lawyer start to prepare a draft contract of sale. Many of the conditions should be standard and the sale price and any specific conditions the purchaser wants to negotiate to include can be added at the time you are ready to sign the contract with the purchaser.

Chapter 10
Life on Your Terms

I wanted to have more time to play and reflect, but I find retirement more stressful than having a nice, steady job because I have to make decisions about where I want to be.

- Walter Cronkite

Retirement can be the most fulfilling and exciting time of your life, but it can also present challenges and uncertainties if it is not planned carefully. In previous years you have been planning and saving for your retirement. Retirement is the time for you to be rewarded with the lifestyle and income you need to enjoy yourself. This hopefully will also be at a time when you have good health and the money to be in a position to make the most of things.

Over the years I have seen many clients who delayed retirement until it was too late for them to enjoy it. When one of the spouses suffers a serious health issue or their elderly parents require extra care, the client then loses the flexibility to travel or enjoy their retirement dreams and goals.

For some it is a big adjustment to stop work and no longer have the business, so they choose to work part-time as they transition to full retirement over a period of time. For other clients the thought of being retired can be overwhelming and they feel lost not having anything to do every day.

Plan for your retirement mentally and financially earlier than just six months before you intend to stop work. Make time to find some hobbies and outside interests and start doing these before you retire. Also, you may want to spend some time away from your partner, as often being home full-time, seven days a week can be overwhelming for both partners. Some interests my clients have undertaken are joining groups like the Men's Shed, volunteering at Meals on Wheels, or camping and travelling.

You may also want to consider using a retirement coach if you find the whole process or the thought of being retired overwhelming. They will help you resolve any issues you have and help you achieve your goals. As we get older sometimes it is difficult trying something new and adjusting to your changed life and routine.

Learn to have a leap of faith, seize the moment, the day and the opportunities which may arrive now that you have time in front of you to try new things. You are on no one's deadline or schedule – if you want to book a cruise or trip away, you are free to go now.

Can I Afford to Retire?

Many clients are afraid they cannot afford to retire. They have heard stories on the news they require $1 million in superannuation by the time they retire.

As discussed in Chapter 6, the Association of Superannuation Funds of Australia (ASFA) recommends that for a couple to have a comfortable retirement they will need an annual income of $60,977 p.a. A lump sum amount of $640,000 will need to be accumulated in your superannuation fund to provide you with this income. This does assume you have no mortgage on your home and you have no other investments in your own name. The assumption is you will draw down all of your capital and receive a part age pension.

ASFA Retirement Standard	Annual living costs	Weekly living costs
Couple - modest	$39,775	$762
Couple - comfortable	$60,977	$1,168
Single - modest	$27,468	$530
Single - comfortable	$43,317	$830

For a single person to have a comfortable retirement, ASFA suggests they will require an income of $43,317 p.a. and they would need to have saved a lump sum amount of $545,000.

ASFA defines a comfortable retirement as one that enables an older, healthy retiree to be involved in a broad range of leisure and recreational activities and have a good standard of living through the purchase of such things as household goods as they arise, be able to pay for private health insurance, have a reasonable car, good clothes, and a range of electronic equipment and the opportunity to do domestic and occasional overseas travel every 18 months to two years.

Each person will have their own goal of what will be a suitable income in retirement. Also, if they want to retire earlier than age 65, e.g. at age 55 or 60, they will need to accumulate a larger lump sum amount. If prior to age 60 they are unable to access their superannuation, it is essential another investment portfolio is established for them to access an income from until they are able to use their superannuation. Several of my clients choose to own an investment property in their personal names which will now provide them a rental income each week/month in their retirement.

Once you have sold the business, collected all outstanding debtors' receipts and finalised payments to staff and their super and all other outstanding creditors you will know the amount remaining for you to use in your retirement planning.

It is a fine line balancing saving tax on the business sale whilst also providing an income for your retirement. If you are under the age of 60, you should consider investing some funds outside of superannuation in your personal name or a family trust, so you can have access to money until you can use your superannuation.

You need to review your budget in retirement and determine how much income you will need to provide you with the lifestyle you want. You should also consider if expenses previously paid by the business, e.g. mobile phone and motor vehicle expenses, will now need to be paid by you personally.

Retirement brings a host of challenges and uncertainties. You will no longer be receiving a regular weekly or fortnightly income from employment and this is the first major adjustment most retirees must make. They will now need to rely on an income from a combination of a pension paid from your superannuation if you are able to access it, other investments held in your personal name, e.g. an investment property, and if eligible, the government age pension.

One of the greatest fears many retirees face heading into retirement is longevity risk – that they will outlive their money and investments. Work with a financial planner to structure a portfolio to ensure you have enough money to live on for the rest of your lives. If you are currently aged 65, as a female, you have a life expectancy of 87 years and as a male, 84 years old. In addition to this, research has shown if you are part of a couple, there is a 50% chance one of you will live to 90+ years.

Your portfolio needs to be structured to allow for your superannuation and investments to pay you and your spouse an annual income for the next 30+ years you are both alive.

If you have reached your preservation age (the age you can access your superannuation) and are now fully retired, this will be a great time for you to start a pension from your superannuation fund.

By commencing a pension from your superannuation, you will be able to convert your super fund into a nil tax environment (assuming you have less than $1.6 million in your account). The money that is invested in your superannuation fund will now pay no tax on the income it earns on investments such as interest income, dividends and the rental income if you own a property in your super fund. The best news is, that you pay no tax on any capital gains made on any assets sold, for example, a rental property or shares that you sell.

When you take a pension payment from your superannuation fund, it will depend on your age if the pension payment will need to be included in your individual tax return. If you are over the age of 60, no pension payments are declared in your tax return.

If you are under the age of 60 then the pension payment must be included in your tax return, but the government allows a 15% tax offset on the taxable portion of the pension. This is all calculated by your superannuation fund and provided to you in a PAYG summary at the end of the financial year.

As you can see when you are 60 and taking a pension from your superannuation fund, this is the sweet spot you want to be. You and your spouse can each have up to $1.6 million invested in superannuation and be paying no tax on the income those investments earn. If these investments had been held in your personal name, you may for the rest of your life be paying tax on those earnings. But don't forget, now that you're no longer working and being paid a wage, you can take advantage of the $18,000 tax free threshold that currently exists as at July 2018.

Let's assume you have $1,000,000 invested in superannuation earning $50,000 which is a 5% return. Below is a comparison on the tax payable by the superannuation fund and you personally if you had held the investment in your name.

Income Earned	Super Fund in Pension (Nil Tax)	Individual (Marginal Tax Rates)
Income earned	$50,000	$50,000
Taxable income	$Nil	$50,000
Tax payable	$Nil	$7,797
Tax benefit each year		$7,797

Let us now look at how your individual tax return would compare if you are under the age of 60 versus over 60 while receiving the pension of $50,000 to keep things simple. We will also assume it is all a taxable component.

Individual Tax Return	Taxpayer Under age 60	Taxpayer Over age 60	Investment in Personal Name (Over age 60)
Pension paid	$50,000	$50,000	$Nil
Taxable income	$50,000	$Nil	$50,000
Tax payable	$7,797	$Nil	$7,797
Add Medicare	$1,000	$Nil	$1,000
Less tax offset on super pension	$7,750	$Nil	$Nil
Net tax payable	$1,047	$Nil	$8,797
Tax saving each year		$1,047	$7,750

Annuities

Another investment to consider in retirement is an annuity and there are several reputable companies in Australia which provide them. To help alleviate the problem of outliving your money companies like Challenger, Macquarie and Colonial provide annuities which you can structure to provide you with guaranteed income payments for the rest of your life, or for a fixed term. The rate of return is fixed when you start the annuity and will not be affected by how investment markets perform or any interest rate movements in the future.

Some of my clients like to use a combination of an annuity, superannuation and, when possible, accessing the age pension to provide them with some stability in the income they will receive in retirement. An annuity can be paid to you monthly, quarterly or even annually and you can choose to index the payments for the Consumer Price Index to reduce the effect of inflation on your annuity pension payments so that the $15,000 annuity income you receive today will maintain its purchasing power in 25 years' time.

There are different features and options to choose with an annuity and if you work with a financial planner, they will be able to run quotes and different scenarios for you to see what suits you and your partner. An annuity can be held in your personal name or in super. If you qualify for the age pension currently any annuities held in your personal name are favourably assessed under the asset test.

Age Pension

Depending on the year you were born you will qualify for the age pension between 65 and 67 years of age. If you or your partner have reached pension age it is worth seeking advice to see if you qualify. To be eligible for the age pension you need to satisfy either the asset test or the income test. The test which gives you the lowest amount of age pension entitlement is the amount you will receive. If you fail to satisfy either the asset test or the income test, then you will not receive any age pension at all. As at 20 September 2018 the thresholds if you would qualify for the age pension were as follows:

Asset Test Thresholds @ 20 September 2018				
	Full Pension	**Home Owner** **Pension** **Cuts Out**	**Non-Home Owner** **Full** **Pension**	**Pension** **cuts out**
Single	$258,500	$564,000	$465,500	$771,000
Couple	$387,500	$848,000	$594,500	$1,055,000
Reduction rate	• The pension is reduced by $78 p.a. per $1,000 of assets over the full pension thresholds			
Indexation	• The full pension thresholds are indexed on 1 July each year in line with CPI			
	• The cut-out thresholds are adjusted 20 March, 1 July and 20 September			

Income Test Thresholds @ 20 September 2018		
	Full Pension	**Pension Cut Out**
Single	$4,472 p.a.	$52,119.60 p.a.
Couple	$7,904 p.a.	$79,736.80 p.a.
Reduction rate	The pension is reduced by $0.50 (singles) and $0.25 (each member of a couple) per $1.00 of income above the full pension thresholds	
Indexation	• The full pension thresholds are indexed on 1 July each year in line with CPI	
	• The cut-out thresholds are adjusted 20 March, 1 July and 20 September	

Please check Centrelink's website for up-to-date threshold amounts and payment amounts.

Some clients are happy to just receive $50 a fortnight from the age pension. The benefit is not limited to the pension payment they receive, but access to the associated benefits of having the concessional health care card which can include reduced council rates, reduced car registration, assistance with your electricity and phone bills depending on which state you live in, travel concessions and not to mention the savings you'll make on your medical prescriptions.

If your plan is to just rely on the age pension for your retirement income, you will not have a comfortable retirement. However, the age pension can help supplement your other income and allow you to draw down less from your own savings.

Maximum Pension Payment Rates @ 20 September 2018	
Pension rate includes pension supplement and energy supplement	
Single	$916.30 per fortnight or $23,823.80 p.a.
Couple per member	$690.70 each per fortnight or $35,916.40 combined p.a.

Make it Happen

You have finally made it to retirement. This is a great time to get creative in achieving your personal goals and items on your bucket list. Maybe you want to:

- start a hobby

- play a sport regularly

- write a book

- visit the children and the grandchildren

- travel locally or overseas

- start a part-time hobby business

- undertake study at university as part of the U3A program

- or??? (insert your wish list item).

If you are wanting to travel, there are a number of creative ways to save money. You may want to consider doing house-sitting or a house swap for holidays in locations you want to visit. You could rent out a spare room in your home or take in a foreign exchange student to earn some extra income in retirement.

Your three action steps for this chapter are:

1. Review your personal budget and determine how much you will need to live on in retirement. It's all great for ASFA to tell you what the average couple will need, but you need to review your own personal situation. Review any debts or loans you still have and work out a plan to repay them as soon as practical and preferably before retirement. My recommendation is for clients to be debt free by the time they retire, so they do not need to worry about meeting any monthly loan repayments.

2. Meet with a financial planner, to review your retirement financial needs and develop a plan on how you will fund your retirement. They will be able to advise if you can access your superannuation, if you qualify for the age pension now or in

the future and what other retirement income products are available which may suit your needs

3. Now is the ideal time to review your personal dreams and goals and take care of your mental well-being. Retirement is an exciting time but also potentially stressful until you find your new routine of not going to work every day and receiving a regular salary. It is time for you to enjoy life and to do all those things you have been postponing.

Chapter 11
Protect Your Empire

Estate planning is an important and everlasting gift you can give your family.
And setting up a smooth inheritance isn't as hard as you might think.

- Suze Orman

Whilst you are busy building your business over the next few years, it is important to implement some strategies to protect your family and the empire you are growing. This chapter will discuss insurances and estate planning and why these are so important to your financial security in the future.

Having the right estate planning structures and insurances in place will allow you to:

- take care of your family and provide them with peace of mind if something happens to you

- provide job security for your employees

- provide security for your suppliers, creditors and customers about the viability of the business (therefore protecting the value of the business which may be sold in the future)

- fund the transfer of ownership to avoid working with previous business partner's spouse

- provide asset protection for you.

In the future if you are injured or were to lose capacity, you can minimise the disruption to your business and your cash flow if you have put the right insurances and documents in place, such as an enduring power of attorney (EPOA).

Insurances are an important part of an estate plan as they allow you to provide your family and your business with some stability should you die or be unable to work because you are injured for a couple of months or become permanently incapacitated.

Many people think estate planning is only about having a will and worrying about what happens to your assets when you die. But estate planning is so much more than just a will. If it is structured correctly, it will provide you with asset protection should your business or you be sued and allow you to separate your personal assets from the business.

Insurances

There are several different types of insurances you can own. The main insurances I will discuss are:

- life insurance

- total and permanent disability insurance

- trauma insurance

- income protection insurance.

You can either apply online these days or meet with a financial planner who can fully assess your needs and requirements for the level of insurance cover you may require. They will consider the level of loans you have and what your future income requirements will be if you were incapacitated to allow you to maintain your family's lifestyle. There needs to be a balance with what you the client can afford to pay, and the level of insurance cover recommended. I am a firm believer it is better for the client to have some insurance cover even at a reduced level, rather than no insurances at all.

Life Insurance

Life insurance, also known as death or term insurance, is self-explanatory. If you pass away, whoever is nominated on the policy, usually your spouse or your estate, will receive a lump sum amount. This money is normally used to reduce any debts the estate may have or to provide your family with a lump sum amount to invest to provide them with the cash to maintain their lifestyle.

In some cases where a client has died their family has been able to use the life insurance proceeds to reduce the debt outstanding on the home mortgage allowing the family to remain in their home where all their fond memories are. Losing a loved one is traumatic enough, but without adequate life insurance your spouse and children will be forced to downsize and move out of the family home if they cannot service the loan. Being unable to remain in the home then becomes an additional traumatic event.

A common mistake people make is only insuring for the level of their loans or debts. You should also allow for an additional lump sum amount to provide your family with some investment income to support them in the first few years after you have passed away. If you pass away, the loss of the steady income from your monthly salary will severely impact the financial budget of your family.

If you have young children and one of the parents is the primary carer and stays home, it is important to have a life insurance policy on that person's life. The life insurance will provide the cash flow to pay for the children to attend day care, hire a nanny or get help around the home. People often underestimate the financial burden of paying for these expenses so the main breadwinner can still go to work and provide for the family.

You can hold the life insurance policy in your personal name or in your superannuation fund. Life insurance premiums paid in your personal name are not tax deductible. However, if the life insurance is held in your superannuation fund, contributing moneys to superannuation to pay the premium, will allow you to claim that contribution as a tax deduction.

Income Protection

If you are injured and unable to work, income protection insurance will provide you with an income to allow you to pay your bills and maintain your lifestyle. Income protection insurance will pay you monthly 75% of the income you are currently earning. You can then use these moneys to meet your loan repayments and other day-to-day cost of living expenses for the family. The insurance companies only provide cover to 75% of your level of income to ensure you have an incentive to return to work and make money.

Your insurance premium will be affected by the usual considerations of your age, occupation, health status and if you are a smoker. The two things clients will adjust to try and reduce their premiums are:

a) Wait period

With income protection, you can vary the wait period on the policies. The wait period is how long you must be off work and sick before the insurance company will start to pay you. You can choose from 14 days, 30 days, 60 days, 90 days and a two year wait period. Generally, I have found most small business owners will choose either a 30 day or 60 day wait period. The longer the wait period generally the cheaper the policy.

b) Benefit period

You also can choose how long you would like the insurance company to have to pay you if you make a claim. It may be for two years, five years, 10 years or to age 60 or 65. It really does depend on your circumstances and what you can afford. The shorter the payment period the lower the premium.

It is generally advisable to hold these policies in your personal name and not in a superannuation fund. The policy held in your personal name will allow you to claim a tax deduction for the premium and when an injury occurs, submitting a claim on the policy is easier and generally quicker than if the policy had been held by a superannuation fund.

However, we don't all live in an ideal world and cash flow can be an issue, especially when you are in the first few years of being in business. It may be advisable initially for you to hold the income protection insurance policy in your superannuation fund.

Another reason not to hold your income protection insurance policy in your superannuation fund is payment of the premiums will have a negative impact on your retirement savings by reducing the balance you will have available to live on when you retire.

However, if it is a matter of choosing to have no income protection insurance cover at all as you cannot afford to pay for this personally, then the preference will be for you to hold the policy in your superannuation fund so you can provide you and your family with some peace of mind should you be injured and unable to work for an extended period of time.

Ensure you review the policy each year, so it remains current and up to date for the level of income you are now earning. For example, a client may have taken out an insurance policy five years ago for $60,000 income. Over the past five years their salary has now increased to $100,000 but they have forgotten to review and increase their income protection insurance policy. If they were now injured and make a claim on the policy, they will only receive 75% of $60,000 ($45,000) and not 75% of $100,000 ($75,000). This will have a huge impact on the family's cash flow requirements while they are unable to work.

Total and Permanent Disability Insurances

According to research conducted by General Reinsurance Life Australia, there is a 10% chance of suffering an illness or injury between the age of 35 and 65 that will lead to total and permanent disability (TPD).

Most people believe that it will not happen to them but the important thing to understand is that it can happen to anyone at any time. Depending on the severity, it could prevent you from ever working again. If you become totally and permanently disabled and you are unable to earn an income, then the TPD insurance provides you with a lump sum to help make modifications to your house and meet medical expenses.

TPD insurance can usually be taken as an addition to your term life policy. It can, however, also be established as standalone cover policy but this will often cost more.

The definitions of TPD can vary between insurers, and it is strongly recommended that you get professional advice from an insurance specialist to find the policy most suitable for you based on your age and occupation.

There are generally two types of TPD options available, "own" occupation or "any" occupation. The purpose of each is as follows:

- own occupation provides a TPD benefit if you are unable to work again in your own occupation

- any occupation provides a TPD benefit if you are unable to work again in any occupation for which you are suited by education, training or experience.

Your premiums for TPD insurance are also affected by factors such as your health, smoking habits and any hazardous activities you engage in, e.g. scuba diving, parachuting or mountain biking.

Total and permanent disability insurance normally should be held in your own name. However, several insurance companies have structured part of the policy to be held in your superannuation fund. This can help you with your personal cash flow by paying part of the premiums from your superannuation contributions and partly from your personal bank account.

Trauma Insurance

An insurance cover not often discussed is trauma insurance. This insurance is paid out on the occurrence of a specific medical condition as defined in your insurance policy. A predefined event that is covered by trauma policy might include a heart attack, cancers (e.g. breast cancer or prostate), a stroke and many other serious medical conditions. In 2017 there was an estimated 134,174 new cases of cancer reported. The good news is, that with improvement in medical treatment the five-year survival rate has increased.

The purpose of this insurance cover is to allow for you to receive a lump sum amount which will assist with medical bills and cover the loss of wages due to time off work for you and your partner as they may need to travel and care for you. This insurance helps reduce the financial burden on the family at this time.

This policy must be held in your personal name and is not tax deductible.

There is no wait period involved with trauma insurance. I had a client diagnosed with prostate cancer who had day surgery to remove the cancer and was back at work within two days. He still received payment of the trauma insurance cover of $150,000.

Clients often complain that insurances are too expensive, and do not see the value of paying premiums for something they may never need to claim on. Having sat beside family members completing the paperwork to lodge the claim when someone has died or is terminally ill, they always are so appreciative their loved one had paid for the insurance cover which would now provide them with peace of mind financially.

Your insurances should be reviewed annually, and as you reduce your debt or your family grows up, you will be able to reduce or even cancel some of them.

Estate Planning

Estate planning is the next important area to consider. Both a will and enduring power of attorney are important documents, plus, there are some other key items you should also review regularly as part of your estate plan.

Will

A will specifies who you wish to inherit your assets on your death. Your will needs to nominate an executor, your beneficiaries and what assets you leave to those beneficiaries.

Many clients do not realise that the assets held in a company or a family trust are not assets of their estate - the only asset that is part of the estate is the shares that they own in the company which owns those assets. Numerous times we see in a will the error of gifting a property owned by a company or a family trust to a beneficiary. Unfortunately, the gift is an "ineffective gift" and the intended beneficiary does not receive their inheritance.

If you have a family trust, and you are the appointor, you can use your will to nominate who will take on the role when you die. The appointor is the person who chooses who can be a trustee of the trust. The trustee has control of the assets in the trust. They decide whether to sell or buy assets in the trust and who will receive the distributions from the trust.

When reviewing your will, it is also a good time for you to consider any binding death benefit nominations (BDBN) or reversionary nominations made in your superannuation fund. You need to ensure that your will is consistent with this. Most people do not realise their superannuation moneys do not form part of their estate and will not automatically be dealt with under their will. Only if a nomination has been made to pay the superannuation proceeds to the estate will it be dealt with under a will.

If you have a blended family, reviewing your superannuation and the BDBN becomes especially important. Recently there has been an increase in the amount of court cases where families have been disputing who is entitled to the money in the superannuation fund and contesting the validity of the BDBN documents.

The legal challenge becomes an added expense to the estate and will reduce the amount available to be distributed to the intended beneficiaries. It will also cause delays in the distribution of all estate moneys to your intended beneficiaries.

If you have a significantly sized estate, you may want to include a provision in your will to set up a testamentary trust. A testamentary trust allows income to be split in a tax effective manner to your beneficiaries. You can determine who you want to control the assets of the testamentary trust in accordance with your wishes. Your beneficiaries will benefit by having income taxed at adult tax rates if they have young children, instead of the penalty minor tax rates. A testamentary trust will also provide asset protection for the surviving spouse and the will makers children if they were adults and working.

Enduring Power of Attorney

An enduring power of attorney is a legal document, which should you lose capacity, your attorney can step in and make decisions for you.

This document is powerful and can be dangerous if not used correctly. It gives power to your attorney to act as if they were you, so they can control your business, your bank accounts and investments. The last thing you would want to happen is to wake up from a coma and find all your bank accounts have been cleaned out. Every state in Australia has different legislation concerning EPOAs, so the state you reside in is where you should have your EPOA document prepared and registered if necessary.

Your nominated attorney should be someone you trust. I recommend clients also nominate a reserve attorney. Your first nominated attorney may be your spouse. If they are unable to act, then your alternate/reserve attorney will step in. You may want to consider a sibling or one of your children if they are over the age of 18, or someone else responsible you trust to act as your attorney. You can even choose to have two or three people act either jointly or separately on your behalf.

Other Issues to Consider

As well as having a will and EPOA, it is important that the following documents are also reviewed regularly if they are relevant to your family:

- copies of the trust deed for any family trust or unit trust you own

- constitutions for the companies you own and operate

- trust deed for a self-managed superannuation fund

- a buy-sell agreement if you are in business with a third party and have one in place.

Clients often forget to advise their lawyers about these entities.

People mistakenly believe if a lawyer has a law degree, they can prepare a will. Unfortunately, succession law (which is about wills and estate planning) has become so complex it is important you talk to someone who has specialised in this area. Some lawyers forget to ask their clients questions about these tax structures or about their superannuation nominations. Consequently, the will that is prepared will be defective in dealing with the very important issue of control of those entities and the assets they own.

Asset Protection

As part of protecting your business and personal assets, it is critical you consider asset protection and what tax structures you should use. If you have a partnership or are a sole trader, you will personally be liable for any debts or injuries that might happen in your business. However, should you have a family trust or company, there will be a degree of separation from that risk and exposure.

Generally, the best asset protection is provided by running your business as a company which provides limited liability. As a director of a company, you will still have legal responsibilities in running the company but overall your personal assets like your home will be protected.

It is important you consider general insurance policies for your business which will protect you as the owner of the business in case an employee has been embezzling or if you are exposed to a cyber-attack and your client's information has been leaked or accessed fraudulently.

Your three action steps for this chapter are:

1. It is important at this stage, to review your business structure. Talk to an accountant if you are a sole trader or in a partnership, to find out if it is the right time for your business to move to a family trust or company. You may find it will be beneficial from a tax planning as well as from an asset protection point of view to remove the risk from your personal name and provide some protection for your home and other personal assets you own.

2. Review your insurances. Look at your personal insurances like life, total and permanent disability insurance, income protection and trauma insurance. Review your business insurances and whether you should consider a buy-sell agreement if you are in business with a third party. Review your cash flow and see if you can afford to pay for the insurances personally or consider other options like holding the policy in superannuation.

3. Review your existing will and EPOA, if you have one. If you do not have a will or EPOA then arrange to have one prepared for you and your spouse. Regularly review your will and EPOA and ensure they stay current with your tax structures and are still in accordance with your wishes about how your assets will be distributed on your death. If you have young children, consider who will be guardian of those children should you pass away.

Afterword

Most financial planners will tell you that the best part of our job is helping clients. A real sense of satisfaction comes from helping clients (who commonly become friends) meet their long-term objectives and achieve the retirement they want.

However, the flip side is that when we meet clients who have invested many years in their business but have not planned nor have the financial rewards to show for their years of hard work, then we feel a little frustrated and sorry for them.

I wrote this book with the intention to help business owners create wealth from their life's work. I have used my extensive experience working with clients in the financial service industry to prepare a "blueprint" that is easy to follow in order to capitalise on owning your own business.

My hope for you is that by reading this book, you take time to look at the "big picture" and with that, implement strategies to increase your savings and profit.

By taking control of your finances and making the time to get educated or meet with professionals like accountants, financial planners and lawyers, your future retirement, regardless whether it will be in five years or 20 years' time, will hopefully be improved. But it is up to you to take action and make a change and implement things.

May your business continue to grow and prosper. I hope you can take advantage of the superannuation system with or without a SMSF. The tax rules are the same for both types of superannuation funds. It does not matter what happens at the next federal election or budget announcements in May each year. Even though some of the financial information in this book will be out of date within six months, the big picture is the same:

- start saving early

- save regularly

- plan ahead

- get advice

- know the tax rules and maximise the deductions to your benefit. For example, if you can make a $25,000 super contribution and can afford it – do it when you can.

If you would like further assistance or wish to connect with me:

Email: info@smsfsa.com.au

Website: www.smsfsa.com.au – register for our free monthly newsletter and download our free e-book.

Facebook: www.facebook.com/SMSFStrategicAdvisors/
www.facebook.com/SBIAustralia/

Appendix 1: Business Plan for (Your Business Name)

VISION

What is your vision about your products and/or services you provide or what problem you solve and for what specific market?

GOALS

	1 Year Goal	3 Year Goal	5 Year Goal
Turnover			
Profit			
Wage to self			
Other goals			

TACTICAL STRATEGIES

QUARTER 1	QUARTER 2	QUARTER 3	QUARTER 4
Key Strategies	Key Strategies	Key Strategies	Key Strategies

ACTION ITEMS

QUARTER 1	QUARTER 2	QUARTER 3	QUARTER 4
January	April	July	October
February	May	August	November
March	June	September	December

Appendix 2: Goal Setting Worksheet

Name:_____   Goal Start Date:_____

My goal is:

_____

_____

_____

_____

Specific	What exactly do I want to achieve? Is the goal clearly written with no ambivalence?	
Measurable	Does the goal answer the questions of how many, how much and/or how often?	
Attainable	Are the results expected realistic? Can I get the support needed to achieve the goal by the target date?	
Relevant	Why am I doing this? Does it matter to me? Is the goal going to significantly make a difference to your business?	
Time-Oriented	Does the goal state a clear and specific completion date?	

Action Item: _____   Who: _____   When: _____

Action Item: _____   Who: _____   When: _____

Action Item: _____   Who: _____   When: _____

Action Item: _____   Who: _____   When: _____

Appendix 3: Personal Budget Planner

Personal Budget Planner

Income $

Your take-home pay		Centrelink benefits	
Your partner's take-home pay		Child support received	
Bonuses / overtime		Other	
Income from savings and investments		**Total Income**	$

Expenses

Home & utilities $		Groceries $	
Mortgage or rent		Supermarket	
Body corporate fees		**Total**	$
Council rates			
Renovations & maintenance		**Personal & medical** $	
Electricity/gas/water		Cosmetics & toiletries	
Internet/phone		Hair & beauty	
Pay TV		Medicines & pharmacy	
Total	$	Dental/doctors/medical	
		Hobbies	
Insurance & financial $		Clothing & shoes	
Car insurance		Computers & gadgets	
Home & contents insurance		Sports & gym	
Personal & life insurance		Pet care & vet	
Health insurance		**Total**	$
Car loan			
Other loans		**Transport & auto** $	
Investments & super contributions		Public transport	
Charity donations		Motor vehicle fuel/rego	
Total	$	Tyres & insurance	
		Total	$
Entertainment & eat-out $		**Children** $	
Coffee/take-aways/lunches		Baby products	
Cigarettes		Childcare	
Drinks & alcohol		Sports & activities	
Restaurants/bars/clubs		School fees	
Books/newspapers & magazines		School uniforms	
Movies & music		Other school needs	
Holidays		Child support payment	
Celebrations & gifts		Other	
Total	$	**Total**	$
		Total Expenses	$
		Surplus/Deficit	$

For an excel worksheet to help you with your budget visit www.moneysmart.gov.au/tools-and-resources/calculators-and-apps/budget-planner

Appendix 4 Cashflow

Cash Flow for [Business name] in [Financial Year]

CASH FLOW	July	August	September	October	November	December	January	February	March	April	May	June
OPENING BALANCE	$0	$0	$0	$0	$0	$0	$0	$0	$0	$0	$0	$0
Cash incoming												
Sales												
Asset sales												
Debtor receipts												
Other income												
Total incoming	$0	$0	$0	$0	$0	$0	$0	$0	$0	$0	$0	$0
Cash outgoing												
Purchases (Stock etc)												
Accountant fees												
Solicitor fees												
Advertising & marketing												
Bank fees & charges												
Interest paid												
Credit card fees												
Utilities (electricity, gas, water)												
Telephone												
Lease/loan payments												
Rent & rates												
Motor vehicle expenses												
Repairs & maintenance												
Stationery & printing												
Membership & affiliation fees												
Licensing												
Insurance												
Superannuation												
Income tax												
Wages (including PAYG)												
More...												
Total outgoing	$0	$0	$0	$0	$0	$0	$0	$0	$0	$0	$0	$0
Monthly cash balance	$0	$0	$0	$0	$0	$0	$0	$0	$0	$0	$0	$0
CLOSING BALANCE	$0	$0	$0	$0	$0	$0	$0	$0	$0	$0	$0	$0

Assumptions:
All figures are GST inclusive.

Appendix 5 Profit and Loss Statement

Profit & Loss for [Business name] as at [Financial Year]

PROFIT & LOSS	July	August	September	October	November	December	January	February	March	April	May	June	Yearly Total
Sales													$0
less cost of goods sold													$0
More...													$0
Gross profit/net sales	$0	$0	$0	$0	$0	$0	$0	$0	$0	$0	$0	$0	$0
Expenses													
Accountant fees													$0
Advertising & marketing													$0
Bank fees & charges													$0
Bank interest													$0
Credit card fees													$0
Utilities (electricity, gas, water)													$0
Telephone													$0
Lease/loan payments													$0
Rent & rates													$0
Motor vehicle expenses													$0
Repairs & maintenance													$0
Stationery & printing													$0
Insurance													$0
Superannuation													$0
Income tax													$0
Wages (including PAYG)													$0
More...													$0
Total expenses	$0	$0	$0	$0	$0	$0	$0	$0	$0	$0	$0	$0	$0
NET PROFIT (Net Income)	$0	$0	$0	$0	$0	$0	$0	$0	$0	$0	$0	$0	$0

Assumptions:

All figures are GST inclusive.

About the Author

Rita was born and raised in Cairns to Italian migrants. Her parents had married in 1965 in Sicily and decided they would come to Australia to set up their home and for a better life. From a young age Rita was exposed to being in a small family business and what that involved. Her father had the local milk run delivering milk to the Cairns Central Business District and everyone in the family had their bit they had to do to help in the business. Whilst Rita and her mother would do the accounts and reconcile the orders each week, her brothers helped with the delivering of milk on school holidays.

After completing her schooling in Cairns, Rita went to Brisbane to complete her Bachelor of Commerce at the University of Queensland. Soon after completing her degree she gained employment with one of the "Big Four" accounting firms in Brisbane in early 1989. This allowed her to then complete her Chartered Accountant qualification with the Institute of Chartered Accountants.

Having returned to Cairns by this stage, at the age of 26 Rita took the leap of faith and went into partnership with Jane Rybarz and so began her first business, Rybarz Zappulla Chartered Accountants. This was the start of a huge learning curve for Rita, to learn how to run a business and manage staff.

The business was successfully sold in 2000 for a nice little profit and it was at this stage Rita decided to become a certified financial planner due to a restraint on her practicing as an accountant for the next three years.

Rita had found her calling. Instead of looking backwards at the numbers and not being able to make a difference for her clients, she could now help them to:

- plan ahead to save money on their income taxes in their business or personal names

- effectively time when they would sell their business or investment properties to minimise the capital gains tax on the sale

- understand the rules of superannuation and plan for their retirement

- achieve their retirement dreams a couple of years later.

In November 2014 the opportunity arose for Rita to again go into business for herself – so SMSF Strategic Advisors was born. As the name states she specialises in providing advice and strategies to self-managed superannuation funds. Rita also assists clients with industry or retail superannuation funds, retirement planning, general financial planning advice, insurance, Centrelink and estate planning strategies.

Rita is a mother to two teenage boys Nicholas and Daniel. She juggles life as a busy mum and running her business. Rita also likes to be actively involved in her community and is a member of the Rotary Club of Cairns Sunrise.

Rita Zappulla is a Certified Financial Planner, Registered Tax Agent and Fellow of Chartered Accountants Australia and New Zealand. SMSF Strategic Advisors, and Rita Zappulla, are both authorised representatives of Synchron AFSL 243313.

Offers

The templates referred to in this book are available to download from our website at

www.smsfsa.com.au/templates

If you have any questions, or would like further information, please email me or visit my website:

Email: info@smsfsa.com.au

Website: www.smsfsa.com.au

Monthly Inspiration

- Subscribe to our monthly newsletter and download our free e-book about superannuation by visiting our website:
www.smsfsa.com.au

- Like us on Facebook to stay up-to-date on the latest news in superannuation and financial planning and upcoming seminars we will be holding:
www.facebook.com/SMSFStrategicAdvisors/
www.facebook.com/SBIAustralia/

One on One

- A personal one-hour meeting with Rita Zappulla in person or by Zoom for $250 (valued at $330). Following the meeting you will be emailed a summary of the issues we discuss.

Full Financial Plan

- Engage to work with Rita and have a full financial plan prepared. Depending on your personal circumstances and following the initial meeting she will be able to provide you with a fixed quote. The price for the initial full financial plan ranges from $3,850 up to $7,700. Monthly payment plans over a six month period are available.

Rita Zappulla is the Principal of SMSF Strategic Advisors and Strategic Business Insights. Rita has over 25 years' experience in the financial services industry having commenced her career as a chartered accountant and now works as a certified financial planner and business coach/mentor. This combination of experience, expertise and qualifications gives Rita a comprehensive understanding of business structures and the Australian tax and superannuation laws. In 2000 Rita began to specialise specifically in the financial planning sector, focusing on self-managed superannuation funds and superannuation advice, retirement planning, estate planning and succession planning.

Rita is passionate about helping small business owners to retire, save tax and to be financially independent for their retirement.

RITA IS AVAILABLE TO SPEAK ON THE FOLLOWING TOPICS:

- How to Plan for an Abundant Retirement;
- The Hidden Secrets with your Super;
- How to buy a property using your Super;
- Estate Planning Made Easy;
- Unlocking Business Tax Structures for Success.

If you wish to invite Rita Zappulla to speak at your event, please email info@smsfsa.com.au.

TESTIMONIALS FROM PEOPLE WHO HAVE ATTENDED OUR SEMINARS:

"Both Rita and Brien are very experienced and knowledgeable in their fields. Their seminars are effectively communicated to deliver highly valuable information for future planning."

~ Anna Rea, Cairns

"Should be more seminars like this to clarify the increasingly complex areas of superannuation and estate planning."

~ Louis Siedle, Cairns

I can thoroughly recommend Rita and Brien – very informative and clearly presented and based on experience so very relevant to anyone approaching retirement (like us!).

~ Nigel Inskip, Cairns

STRATEGIC
BUSINESS
INSIGHTS

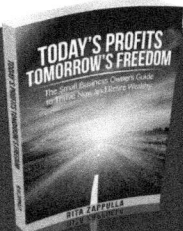

TODAY'S PROFITS
TOMORROW'S FREEDOM

(07) 4225 5428
info@smsfsa.com.au
www.smsfsa.com.au
P O Box 552 Cairns QLD 4870

www.ingramcontent.com/pod-product-compliance
Lightning Source LLC
Chambersburg PA
CBHW031858200326
41597CB00012B/459